D0610783

A WINDOW
ON THE UNIVERSE

Tales of wonder are as old as the hills. Ever since story-telling began there have been tales of gods, devils, and hobgoblins, tales of the sun, the moon, the stars. Surrounded by the great mystery of the universe, humankind has sought to make sense of it all by ingenious explanations and imaginative ideas that range far beyond what can be seen or heard or touched.

Science-fiction stories are the tales of wonder for our age. Instead of winged horses, witches, and golden palaces, we have spacecraft, the minds of alien creatures, and remote planets. How will we deal with alien life-forms inhabiting a human body, or launching a war against us from outer space? Will we go mad or become extinct because of the machines that we have invented, or will we be destroyed by an asteroid colliding with Earth? These stories send us travelling through time and space, confronting us with new dangers, new uncertainties, new dilemmas. Above all, they remind us that human beings are only very small pebbles on a very big beach.

The English poet Tennyson once wrote:

For I dipped into the future, far as human eye could see,
Saw the vision of the world, and all the wonder that would
be . . .

So let us dip into the future . . .

OXFORD BOOKWORMS COLLECTION

Acknowledgements

The editors and publishers are grateful for permission to use the following copyright material:

'Who Can Replace a Man?' from *The Canopy of Time* by BRIAN ALDISS, published by Faber & Faber Ltd 1959. Copyright © Brian Aldiss 1959. Reprinted by permission of Curtis Brown Group Ltd.

'The Machine That Won the War' by ISAAC ASIMOV. Copyright © 1961 by Mercury Press Inc. From *Nightfall and other Stories* by Isaac Asimov. Reprinted by permission of Doubleday, a division of Bantam Doubleday Dell Publishing Group Inc.

'Zero Hour' from *The Illustrated Man* by RAY BRADBURY. Reprinted by permission of the Peters Fraser & Dunlop Group Ltd.

'The Hammer of God' by ARTHUR C. CLARKE, first published in *Time*, Fall 1992. Reprinted by permission of David Higham Associates Ltd.

'The Sound Machine' from *Someone Like You* by ROALD DAHL, published by Michael Joseph Ltd and Penguin Books Ltd. Reprinted by permission of Murray Pollinger.

'Human Is' by PHILIP K. DICK from *Second Variety: Volume 2 of the Collected Stories of Philip K. Dick*. Reprinted by permission of the author and the author's agents, Scovil Chichak Galen Literary Agency Inc, New York.

'Stitch in Time' from *Consider Her Ways and Others* by JOHN WYNDHAM, published by Michael Joseph Ltd 1961. Reprinted by permission of David Higham Associates Ltd.

The publishers have made every effort to trace the copyright holders of the following stories and would be pleased to hear from them:

'It's a *Good* Life' by JEROME BIXBY, reprinted in *Best SF Four* published by Faber & Faber Ltd 1960.

'The Star Ducks' by BILL BROWN, first published in *The Magazine of Fantasy and Science Fiction*, reprinted in *Best SF Six* published by Faber & Faber Ltd 1966.

THE EDITOR would like to thank Andy Sawyer of the Science Fiction Foundation Collection, University of Liverpool Library, for his help in researching biographical information on the authors in this volume.

A WINDOW
ON THE UNIVERSE

Short Stories

EDITED BY
Jennifer Bassett

SERIES ADVISERS
H.G. Widdowson
Jennifer Bassett

OXFORD UNIVERSITY PRESS

OXFORD
UNIVERSITY PRESS

Great Clarendon Street, Oxford OX2 6DP

Oxford University Press is a department of the University of Oxford.
It furthers the University's objective of excellence in research, scholarship,
and education by publishing worldwide in

Oxford New York

Auckland Cape Town Dar es Salaam Hong Kong Karachi
Kuala Lumpur Madrid Melbourne Mexico City Nairobi
New Delhi Shanghai Taipei Toronto

With offices in

Argentina Austria Brazil Chile Czech Republic France Greece
Guatemala Hungary Italy Japan Poland Portugal Singapore
South Korea Switzerland Thailand Turkey Ukraine Vietnam

OXFORD and OXFORD ENGLISH are registered trade marks of
Oxford University Press in the UK and in certain other countries

This edition © Oxford University Press 2010

Database right Oxford University Press (maker)

First published 1995

12 14 16 18 20 19 17 15 13

ISBN: 978 0 19 422694 3

Typeset by Pentacor Plc, High Wycombe, Bucks

Printed in China

Illustrated by: Susan Scott

OXFORD BOOKWORMS
～ COLLECTION ～

FOREWORD

Texts of all kinds, including literary texts, are used as data for language teaching. They are designed or adapted and pressed into service to exemplify the language and provide practice in reading. These are commendable pedagogic purposes. They are not, however, what authors or readers of texts usually have in mind. The reason we read something is because we feel the writer has something of interest or significance to say and we only attend to the language to the extent that it helps us to understand what that might be. An important part of language learning is knowing how to adopt this normal reader role, how to use language to achieve meanings of significance to us, and so make texts our own.

The purpose of the *Oxford Bookworms Collection* is to encourage students of English to adopt this role. It offers samples of English language fiction, unabridged and unsimplified, which have been selected and presented to induce enjoyment, and to develop a sensitivity to the language through an appreciation of the literature. The intention is to stimulate students to find in fiction what Jane Austen found: 'the most thorough knowledge of human nature, the happiest delineation of its varieties, the liveliest effusions of wit and humour ... conveyed to the world in the best chosen language.' *(Northanger Abbey)*

H. G. Widdowson
Series Adviser

OXFORD BOOKWORMS
∼ COLLECTION ∼

None of the texts has been abridged or simplified in any way, but each volume contains notes and questions to help students in their understanding and appreciation.

Before each story
- a short biographical note on the author
- an introduction to the theme and characters of the story

After each story
- NOTES

  Some words and phrases in the texts are marked with an asterisk*, and explanations for these are given in the notes. The expressions selected are usually cultural references or archaic and dialect words unlikely to be found in dictionaries. Other difficult words are not explained. This is because to do so might be to focus attention too much on the analysis of particular meanings, and to disrupt the natural reading process. Students should be encouraged by their engagement with the story to infer general and relevant meaning from context.

- DISCUSSION

  These are questions on the story's theme and characters, designed to stimulate class discussion or to encourage the individual reader to think about the story from different points of view.

- LANGUAGE FOCUS

  Some of these questions and tasks direct the reader's attention to particular features of language use or style; others focus on specific meanings and their significance in the story.

- ACTIVITIES

  These are suggestions for creative writing activities, to encourage readers to explore or develop the themes of the story in various imaginative ways.

- QUESTIONS FOR DISCUSSION OR WRITING

  These are questions (sometimes under the heading 'Ideas for Comparison Activities') with ideas for discussion or writing which compare and contrast a number of stories in the volume.

CURRENT TITLES

From the Cradle to the Grave	**The Eye of Childhood**
Crime Never Pays	**And All for Love . . .**
A Window on the Universe	**A Tangled Web**

Contents

ZERO HOUR

THE AUTHOR

Ray Bradbury was born in 1920 in Illinois, USA, and became a full-time writer in 1943. His reputation as a leading writer of science fiction was established with *The Martian Chronicles*, a series of interwoven stories about attempts by humans to colonize Mars. Another of his well-known works is the novel *Fahrenheit 451*, which is set in a totalitarian future when books are burned because ideas are dangerous. This was later made into a film by François Truffaut. Among Bradbury's many collections of short stories are *The Illustrated Man*, *The Golden Apples of the Sun*, and *The Day It Rained Forever*.

THE STORY

Children have fertile imaginations. They can move between fantasy and reality without telling the difference between them. Sometimes they invent imaginary friends with whom they play and talk and argue, as though it were the most natural thing in the world. Perhaps they need this freedom of the imagination, living as they do under the inexplicable tyranny of adult rules and restrictions.

In a world that is technologically self-confident and at peace with itself, Mink plays happily with her friends in front of the house. Energetic and forceful, she instructs the others in their roles. From a window her mother watches, amused, tolerant. It is rather a mysterious game, though, with an air of urgency about it, a sense of purpose not quite in keeping with the peaceful city afternoon . . .

ZERO HOUR

Oh, it was to be so jolly! What a game! Such excitement they hadn't known in years. The children catapulted this way and that across the green lawns, shouting at each other, holding hands, flying in circles, climbing trees, laughing. Overhead the rockets flew, and beetle cars whispered by on the streets, but the children played on. Such fun, such tremulous joy, such tumbling and hearty screaming.

Mink ran into the house, all dirt and sweat. For her seven years she was loud and strong and definite. Her mother, Mrs Morris, hardly saw her as she yanked out drawers and rattled pans and tools into a large sack.

'Heavens, Mink, what's going on?'

'The most exciting game ever!' gasped Mink, pink-faced.

'Stop and get your breath,' said the mother.

'No, I'm all right,' gasped Mink. 'Okay I take these things, Mom?'

'But don't dent them,' said Mrs Morris.

'Thank you, thank you!' cried Mink, and boom! she was gone, like a rocket.

Mrs Morris surveyed the fleeing tot. 'What's the name of the game?'

'Invasion!' said Mink. The door slammed.

In every yard on the street children brought out knives and forks and pokers and old stovepipes and can-openers.

It was an interesting fact that this fury and bustle occurred only among the younger children. The older ones, those ten years and more, disdained the affair and marched scornfully off on hikes or played a more dignified version of hide-and-seek on their own.

Meanwhile, parents came and went in chromium beetles. Repairmen came to repair the vacuum elevators in houses, to fix fluttering

television sets or hammer upon stubborn food-delivery tubes. The
adult civilization passed and repassed the busy youngsters, jealous
of the fierce energy of the wild tots, tolerantly amused at their
flourishings, longing to join in themselves.

'This and this and *this*,' said Mink, instructing the others with
their assorted spoons and wrenches. 'Do that, and bring *that* over
here. No! *Here*, ninny! Right. Now, get back while I fix this.' Tongue
in teeth, face wrinkled in thought. 'Like that. See?'

'Yayyyy!' shouted the kids.

Twelve-year-old Joseph Connors ran up.

'Go away,' said Mink straight at him.

'I wanna play,' said Joseph.

'Can't!' said Mink.

'Why not?'

'You'd just make fun of us.'

'Honest, I wouldn't.'

'No. We know *you*. Go away or we'll kick you.'

Another twelve-year-old boy whirred by on little motor skates.
'Hey, Joe! Come on! Let them sissies play!'

Joseph showed reluctance and a certain wistfulness. 'I *want* to
play,' he said.

'You're old,' said Mink firmly.

'Not *that* old,' said Joe sensibly.

'You'd only laugh and spoil the Invasion.'

The boy on the motor skates made a rude lip noise. 'Come on,
Joe! Them and their fairies! Nuts!'

Joseph walked off slowly. He kept looking back, all down the
block.

Mink was already busy again. She made a kind of apparatus with
her gathered equipment. She had appointed another little girl with
a pad and pencil to take down notes in painful slow scribbles. Their
voices rose and fell in the warm sunlight.

All around them the city hummed. The streets were lined with good green and peaceful trees. Only the wind made a conflict across the city, across the country, across the continent. In a thousand other cities there were trees and children and avenues, business men in their quiet offices taping their voices, or watching televisors. Rockets hovered like darning needles in the blue sky. There was the universal, quiet conceit and easiness of men accustomed to peace, quite certain there would never be trouble again. Arm in arm, men all over earth were a united front. The perfect weapons were held in equal trust by all nations. A situation of incredibly beautiful balance had been brought about. There were no traitors among men, no unhappy ones, no disgruntled ones; therefore the world was based upon a stable ground. Sunlight illumined half the world and the trees drowsed in a tide of warm air.

Mink's mother, from her upstairs window, gazed down.

The children. She looked upon them and shook her head. Well, they'd eat well, sleep well, and be in school on Monday. Bless their vigorous little bodies. She listened.

Mink talked earnestly to someone near the rose bush – though there was no one there.

These odd children. And the little girl, what was her name? Anna? Anna took notes on a pad. First, Mink asked the rose bush a question, then called the answer to Anna.

'Triangle,' said Mink.

'What's a tri,' said Anna with difficulty, 'angle?'

'Never mind,' said Mink.

'How you spell it?' asked Anna.

'T-r-i—' spelled Mink slowly, then snapped, 'Oh, spell it yourself!' She went on to other words. 'Beam,' she said.

'I haven't got tri,' said Anna, 'angle down yet!'

'Well, hurry, hurry!' cried Mink.

Mink's mother leaned out of the upstairs window. 'A-n-g-l-e,' she spelled down at Anna.

'Oh, thanks, Mrs Morris,' said Anna.

'Certainly,' said Mink's mother and withdrew, laughing, to dust the hall with an electro-duster magnet.

The voices wavered on the shimmery air. 'Beam,' said Anna. Fading.

'Four-nine-seven-A-and-B-and-X,' said Mink, far away, seriously. 'And a fork and a string and a – hex-hex-agony – hexagon*al*!'

At lunch Mink gulped milk at one toss and was at the door. Her mother slapped the table.

'You sit right back down,' commanded Mrs Morris. 'Hot soup in a minute.' She poked a red button on the kitchen butler, and ten seconds later something landed with a bump in the rubber receiver. Mrs Morris opened it, took out a can with a pair of aluminium holders, unsealed it with a flick, and poured hot soup into a bowl.

During all this Mink fidgeted. 'Hurry, Mom! This is a matter of life and death! Aw—'

'I was the same way at your age. Always life and death. I know.'

Mink banged away at the soup.

'Slow down,' said Mom.

'Can't,' said Mink. 'Drill's waiting for me.'

'Who's Drill? What a peculiar name,' said Mom.

'You don't know him,' said Mink.

'A new boy in the neighbourhood?' asked Mom.

'He's new all right,' said Mink. She started on her second bowl.

'Which one is Drill?' asked Mom.

'He's around,' said Mink, evasively. 'You'll make fun. Everybody pokes fun. Gee, darn.'

'Is Drill shy?'

'Yes. No. In a way. Gosh, Mom, I got to run if we want to have the Invasion!'

'Who's invading what?'

'Martians invading Earth. Well, not exactly Martians. They're – I don't know. From up.' She pointed with her spoon.

'And *inside*,' said Mom, touching Mink's feverish brow.

Mink rebelled. 'You're laughing! You'll kill Drill and everybody.'

'I didn't mean to,' said Mom. 'Drill's a Martian?'

'No. He's – well – maybe from Jupiter or Saturn or Venus. Anyway, he's had a hard time.'

'I imagine.' Mrs Morris hid her mouth behind her hand.

'They couldn't figure a way to attack Earth.'

'We're impregnable,' said Mom in mock seriousness.

'That's the word Drill used! Impreg— That was the word, Mom.'

'My, my, Drill's a brilliant little boy. Two-bit words.'

'They couldn't figure a way to attack, Mom. Drill says – he says in order to make a good fight you got to have a new way of surprising people. That way you win. And he says also you got to have help from your enemy.'

'A fifth column,' said Mom.

'Yeah. That's what Drill said. And they couldn't figure a way to surprise Earth or get help.'

'No wonder. We're pretty darn strong.' Mom laughed, cleaning up. Mink sat there, staring at the table, seeing what she was talking about.

'Until, one day,' whispered Mink melodramatically, 'they thought of children!'

'*Well!*' said Mrs Morris brightly.

'And they thought of how grown-ups are so busy they never look under rose bushes or on lawns!'

'Only for snails and fungus.'

'And then there's something about dim-dims.'

'Dim-dims?'

'Dimens-shuns.'

'Dimensions?'

'Four of 'em! And there's something about kids under nine and imagination. It's real funny to hear Drill talk.'

Mrs Morris was tired. 'Well, it must be funny. You're keeping Drill waiting now. It's getting late in the day and, if you want to have your Invasion before your supper bath, you'd better jump.'

'Do I have to take a bath?' growled Mink.

'You do! Why is it children hate water? No matter what age you live in children hate water behind the ears!'

'Drill says I won't have to take baths,' said Mink.

'Oh, he does, does he?'

'He told all the kids that. No more baths. And we can stay up till ten o'clock and go to two televisor shows on Saturday 'stead of one!'

'Well, Mr Drill better mind his p's and q's. I'll call up his mother and—'

Mink went to the door. 'We're having trouble with guys like Pete Britz and Dale Jerrick. They're growing up. They make fun. They're worse than parents. They just won't believe in Drill. They're so snooty, 'cause they're growing up. You'd think they'd know better. They were little only a coupla years ago. I hate them worst. We'll kill them *first*.'

'Your father and me last?'

'Drill says you're dangerous. Know why? 'Cause you don't believe in Martians! They're going to let *us* run the world. Well, not just us, but the kids over in the next block, too. I might be queen.' She opened the door.

'Mom?'

'Yes?'

'What's lodge-ick?'

'Logic? Why, dear, logic is knowing what things are true and not true.'

'He *mentioned* that,' said Mink. 'And what's im-pres-sion-able?'

It took her a minute to say it.

'Why, it means . . .' Her mother looked at the floor, laughing gently. 'It means – to be a child, dear.'

'Thanks for lunch!' Mink ran out, then stuck her head back in. 'Mom, I'll be sure you won't be hurt much, really!'

'Well, thanks,' said Mom.

Slam went the door.

At four o'clock the audio-visor buzzed. Mrs Morris flipped the tab. 'Hello, Helen!' she said in welcome.

'Hello, Mary. How are things in New York?'

'Fine. How are things in Scranton? You look tired.'

'So do you. The children. Underfoot,' said Helen.

Mrs Morris sighed. 'My Mink too. The super-Invasion.'

Helen laughed. 'Are your kids playing that game too?'

'Lord, yes. Tomorrow it'll be geometrical jacks and motorized hopscotch. Were we this bad when we were kids in '48?'

'Worse. Japs and Nazis*. Don't know how my parents put up with me. Tomboy.'

'Parents learn to shut their ears.'

A silence.

'What's wrong, Mary?' asked Helen.

Mrs Morris's eyes were half closed; her tongue slid slowly, thoughtfully, over her lower lip. 'Eh?' She jerked. 'Oh, nothing. Just thought about *that*. Shutting ears and such. Never mind. Where were we?'

'My boy Tim's got a crush on some guy named – *Drill*, I think it was.'

'Must be a new password. Mink likes him too.'

'Didn't know it had got as far as New York. Word of mouth, I imagine. Looks like a scrap drive*. I talked to Josephine and she said her kids – that's in Boston – are wild on this new game. It's sweeping the country.'

At this moment Mink trotted into the kitchen to gulp a glass of water. Mrs Morris turned. 'How're things going?'

'Almost finished,' said Mink.

'Swell,' said Mrs Morris. 'What's *that*?'

'A yo-yo,' said Mink. 'Watch.'

She flung the yo-yo down its string. Reaching the end it—

It vanished.

'See?' said Mink. 'Ope!' Dibbling her finger, she made the yo-yo reappear and zip up the string.

'Do that again,' said her mother.

'Can't. Zero hour's five o'clock. Bye!' Mink exited, zipping her yo-yo.

On the audio-visor, Helen laughed. 'Tim brought one of those yo-yos in this morning, but when I got curious he said he wouldn't show it to me, and when I tried to work it, finally, it wouldn't work.'

'You're not *impressionable*,' said Mrs Morris.

'What?'

'Never mind. Something I thought of. Can I help you, Helen?'

'I wanted to get that black-and-white cake recipe . . .'

The hour drowsed by. The day waned. The sun lowered in the peaceful blue sky. Shadows lengthened on the green lawns. The laughter and excitement continued. One little girl ran away, crying. Mrs Morris came out the front door.

'Mink, was that Peggy Ann crying?'

Mink was bent over in the yard, near the rose bush. 'Yeah. She's a scarebaby*. We won't let her play, now. She's getting too old to play. I guess she grew up all of a sudden.'

'Is that why she cried? Nonsense. Give me a civil answer, young lady, or inside you come!'

Mink whirled in consternation, mixed with irritation. 'I can't quit now. It's almost time. I'll be good. I'm sorry.'

'Did you hit Peggy Ann?'

'No, honest. You ask her. It was something – well, she's just a scaredy pants*.'

The ring of children drew in around Mink where she scowled at her work with spoons and a kind of square-shaped arrangement of hammers and pipes. 'There and there,' murmured Mink.

'What's wrong?' said Mrs Morris.

'Drill's stuck. Half-way. If we could only get him all the way through it'd be easier. Then all the others could come through after him.'

'Can I help?'

'No'm, thanks. I'll fix it.'

'All right. I'll call you for your bath in half an hour. I'm tired of watching you.'

She went in and sat in the electric relaxing chair, sipping a little beer from a half-empty glass. The chair massaged her back. Children, children. Children and love and hate, side by side. Sometimes children loved you, hated you – all in half a second. Strange children, did they ever forget or forgive the whippings and the harsh, strict words of command? She wondered. How can you ever forget or forgive those over and above you, those tall and silly dictators?

Time passed. A curious, waiting silence came upon the street, deepening.

Five o'clock. A clock sang softly somewhere in the house in a quiet musical voice: 'Five o'clock – five o'clock. Time's a-wasting. Five o'clock,' and purred away into silence.

Zero hour.

Mrs Morris chuckled in her throat. Zero hour.

A beetle car hummed into the driveway. Mr Morris. Mrs Morris smiled. Mr Morris got out of the beetle, locked it, and called hello to Mink at her work. Mink ignored him. He laughed and stood for a moment watching the children. Then he walked up the front steps.

'Hello, darling.'

'Hello, Henry.'

She strained forward on the edge of the chair, listening. The children were silent. Too silent.

He emptied his pipe, refilled it. 'Swell day. Makes you glad to be alive.'

Buzz.

'What's that?' asked Henry.

'I don't know.' She got up suddenly, her eyes widening. She was going to say something. She stopped it. Ridiculous. Her nerves jumped. 'Those children haven't anything dangerous out there, have they?' she said.

'Nothing but pipes and hammers. Why?'

'Nothing electrical?'

'Heck, no,' said Henry. 'I looked.'

She walked to the kitchen. The buzzing continued. 'Just the same, you'd better go tell them to quit. It's after five. Tell them—' Her eyes widened and narrowed. 'Tell them to put off their Invasion until tomorrow.' She laughed, nervously.

The buzzing grew louder.

'What are they up to? I'd better go look, all right.'

The explosion!

The house shook with dull sound. There were other explosions in other yards on other streets.

Involuntarily, Mrs Morris screamed. 'Up this way!' she cried senselessly, knowing no sense, no reason. Perhaps she saw something from the corners of her eyes; perhaps she smelled a new odour or heard a new noise. There was no time to argue with Henry to convince him. Let him think her insane. Yes, insane! Shrieking, she ran upstairs. He ran after her to see what she was up to. 'In the attic!' she screamed. 'That's where it is!' It was only a poor excuse to get him in the attic in time. Oh, God – in time!

Another explosion outside. The children screamed with delight, as if at a great fireworks display.

'It's not in the attic!' cried Henry. 'It's outside!'

'No, no!' Wheezing, gasping, she fumbled at the attic door. 'I'll show you. Hurry! I'll show you!'

They tumbled into the attic. She slammed the door, locked it, took the key, threw it into a far, cluttered corner.

She was babbling wild stuff now. It came out of her. All the subconscious suspicion and fear that had gathered secretly all afternoon and fermented like a wine in her. All the little revelations and knowledges and sense that had bothered her all day and which she had, logically and carefully and sensibly, rejected and censored. Now it exploded in her and shook her to bits.

'There, there,' she said, sobbing against the door. 'We're safe until tonight. Maybe we can sneak out. Maybe we can escape!'

Henry blew up too, but for another reason. 'Are you crazy? Why'd you throw that key away? Damn it, honey!'

'Yes, yes, I'm crazy, if it helps, but stay here with me!'

'I don't know how in hell I *can* get out!'

'Quiet. They'll hear us. Oh, God, they'll find us soon enough—'

Below them, Mink's voice. The husband stopped. There was a great universal humming and sizzling, a screaming and giggling. Downstairs the audio-televisor buzzed and buzzed insistently, alarmingly, violently. *Is that Helen calling?* thought Mrs Morris. *And is she calling about what I think she's calling about?*

Footsteps came into the house. Heavy footsteps.

'Who's coming in my house?' demanded Henry angrily. 'Who's tramping around down there?'

Heavy feet. Twenty, thirty, forty, fifty of them. Fifty persons crowding into the house. The humming. The giggling of the children. 'This way!' cried Mink, below.

'Who's downstairs?' roared Henry. 'Who's there?'

'Hush. Oh, nonononononono!' said his wife weakly, holding him. 'Please, be quiet. They might go away.'

'Mom?' called Mink. 'Dad?' A pause. 'Where are you?'

Heavy footsteps, heavy, heavy, very *heavy* footsteps, came up the stairs. Mink leading them.

'Mom?' A hesitation. 'Dad?' A waiting, a silence.

Humming. Footsteps towards the attic. Mink's first.

They trembled together in silence in the attic, Mr and Mrs Morris. For some reason the electric humming, the queer cold light suddenly visible under the door crack, the strange odour and the alien sound of eagerness in Mink's voice finally got through to Henry Morris too. He stood, shivering, in the dark silence, his wife beside him.

'Mom! Dad!'

Footsteps. A little humming sound. The attic-lock melted. The door opened. Mink peered inside, tall blue shadows behind her.

'Peekaboo*,' said Mink.

NOTES

Japs and Nazis (p16)

    (offensive) terms used for the Japanese and German enemy during the
    Second World War

scrap drive (p16)

    a collection of useless pieces of old metal

scarebaby / scaredy pants (p17/18)

    childish words for an easily frightened person

peekaboo (p21)

    a word used in children's games when looking out of a hiding-place

DISCUSSION

1   To Mink, helping the aliens to invade Earth seems to be just an
exciting game. Do you think this is realistic in a seven-year-old child?
Why does Mink tell her mother all about the coming invasion? Are there
suggestions anywhere in the story that Mink has at least some idea of
the significance of an invasion and of what Drill has apparently told
her?

2   Do you think Mrs Morris is shown as a careful, sensible kind of
mother? Should she have realized earlier that something very strange
was going on? What are the clues that she could have picked up from
Mink, or her friend Helen in New York? And what conclusions could
she have drawn?

3   How much information is given in the story about the nature and
appearance of the invading aliens? Do you think the ending of the
story would have been more effective if the description had been more
detailed than just 'tall blue shadows' behind Mink? Why, or why not?

4   The story is set in a world that is apparently very different from the
one we know today. Do you think such a harmonious society is a likely
future, or is the picture far too optimistic?

LANGUAGE FOCUS

1   The following list of appliances and machines, mentioned in passing
in the story to create a futuristic setting, are mostly existing words
used in combination to suggest new meanings and new inventions – a

common device in science-fiction writing. These words, being invented, will not be found in dictionaries, and we are not expected to know precisely what they mean. But what meanings do they suggest to you? Use your imagination, and your knowledge of the component words, to describe the appearance or purpose of the items.

beetle cars (p10)
vacuum elevators (p10)
food-delivery tubes (p11)
motor skates (p11)
televisor (p12)
electro-duster magnet (p13)
kitchen butler (p13)
audio-visor (p16)
electric relaxing chair (p18)

2 There are several words used by Mink which are very unlikely words for a seven-year-old to use. Which are they? Two of them, *logic* and *impressionable*, Mrs Morris attempts to explain to Mink. How would you define them, and the other 'difficult' words that Mink uses? What effect do these words have in the story?

ACTIVITIES

1 Imagine that Mrs Morris realized much earlier that the invasion was not just a childish game. Invent a conversation between her and Mink, as Mrs Morris tries both to get more information from Mink, and to persuade her that Drill is not a nice friend to have.

2 The story ends at a moment of high tension. What event does the author imply will happen next? And what do you think will happen to the children? Will the invaders be benign, and uphold their promises of no more baths, staying up till ten o'clock, and two televisor shows on Saturdays? Write another paragraph to describe the results of the invasion.

THE STAR DUCKS

THE AUTHOR

Bill Brown was born in 1910 in Oregon, USA. He worked as a journalist, a park ranger, and a teacher of creative writing. As a young man in the 1930s, he made a voyage in a thirty-two foot schooner through the South Seas, and during World War II descended a Himalayan river by rubber boat. Two of his books, *Uncharted Voyage* and *Roaring River*, are based on these adventures. His story *The Star Ducks* was published in 1950 in the magazine *Fantasy and Science Fiction*. Three more science-fiction stories followed: *The Tronk and the Trumpet, Medicine Dancer*, and *Spunk Water*. He died in 1964.

THE STORY

There is no reason to suppose that Earth is the only planet in the universe capable of supporting life in some form or other. Until we can communicate with other galaxies, however, we can only speculate and imagine. Science fiction offers us a rich range of alien life-forms, from the sublime to the ridiculous, and at the same time often shows humankind from a new, and sometimes unflattering, angle.

The merest hint of a visitation from outer space and reporter Ward Rafferty would rush to the scene, keen to be the first with a sensational scoop for his newspaper. The Alsops, on the other hand, are untroubled by the thought of wonders from space. They pursue their humdrum lives as farmers, raising chickens, milking the cows, doing a bit of friendly trade with any visitors that happen to drop by . . .

THE STAR DUCKS

Ward Rafferty's long, sensitive newshawk's nose alerted him for a hoax as soon as he saw the old Alsop place. There was no crowd of curious farmers standing around, no ambulance.

Rafferty left *The Times* press car under a walnut tree in the drive and stood for a moment noting every detail with the efficiency that made him *The Times*' top reporter. The old Alsop house was brown, weathered, two-storey with cream-coloured filigree around the windows and a lawn that had grown up to weeds. Out in back were the barn and chicken houses and fences that were propped up with boards and pieces of pipe. The front gate was hanging by one hinge but it could be opened by lifting it. Rafferty went in and climbed the steps, careful for loose boards.

Mr Alsop came out on the porch to meet him. 'Howdy do,' he said.

Rafferty pushed his hat back on his head the way he always did before he said: 'I'm Rafferty of *The Times*.' Most people knew his by-line and he liked to watch their faces when he said it.

'Rafferty?' Mr Alsop said, and Rafferty knew he wasn't a *Times* reader.

'I'm a reporter,' Rafferty said. 'Somebody phoned in and said an airplane cracked up around here.'

Mr Alsop looked thoughtful and shook his head slowly.

'No,' he said.

Rafferty saw right away that Alsop was a slow thinker so he gave him time, mentally pegging him a taciturn Yankee*. Mr Alsop answered again, 'Noooooooooooooo.'

The screen door squeaked and Mrs Alsop came out. Since Mr Alsop was still thinking, Rafferty repeated the information for Mrs Alsop, thinking she looked a little brighter than her husband. But

Mrs Alsop shook her head and said, 'Noooooooooooo,' in exactly the same tone Mr Alsop had used.

Rafferty turned around with his hand on the porch railing ready to go down the steps.

'I guess it was a phony tip,' he said. 'We get lots of them. Somebody said an airplane came down in your field this morning, straight down trailing fire.'

Mrs Alsop's face lighted up. 'Ohhhhhhhhhh!' she said. 'Yes, it did but it wasn't wrecked. Besides, it isn't really an airplane. That is, it doesn't have wings on it.'

Rafferty stopped with his foot in the air over the top step. 'I beg your pardon?' he said. 'An airplane came down? And it didn't have wings?'

'Yes,' Mrs Alsop said. 'It's out there in the barn now. It belongs to some folks who bend iron with a hammer.'

This, Rafferty thought, begins to smell like news again.

'Oh, a helicopter,' he said.

Mrs Alsop shook her head. 'No, I don't think it is. It doesn't have any of those fans. But you can go out to the barn and have a look. Take him out, Alfred. Tell him to keep on the walk because it's muddy.'

'Come along,' Mr Alsop said brightly. 'I'd like to look the contraption over again myself.'

Rafferty followed Mr Alsop around the house on the board walk thinking he'd been mixed up with some queer people in his work, some crackpots and some screwballs, some imbeciles and some lunatics, but for sheer dumbness, these Alsops had them all beat.

'Got a lot of chickens this year,' Mr Alsop said. 'All fine stock. Minorcas. Sent away for roosters and I've built a fine flock. But do you think chickens'll do very well up on a star, Mr Rafferty?'

Rafferty involuntarily looked up at the sky and stepped off the boards into the mud.

'Up on a what?'

'I said up on a star.' Mr Alsop had reached the barn door and was trying to shove it open. 'Sticks,' he said. Rafferty put his shoulder to it and the door slid. When it was open a foot, Rafferty looked inside and he knew he had a story.

The object inside looked like a giant plastic balloon only half inflated so that it was globular on top and its flat bottom rested on the straw-covered floor. It was just small enough to go through the barn door. Obviously it was somebody's crackpot idea of a space ship, Rafferty thought. The headline that flashed across his mind in thirty-six point Bodoni* was 'Local Farmer Builds Rocket Ship For Moon Voyage'.

'Mr Alsop,' Rafferty said hopefully, 'you didn't build this thing, did you?'

Mr Alsop laughed. 'Oh, no, I didn't build it. I wouldn't know how to build one of those things. Some friends of ours came in it. Gosh, I wouldn't even know how to fly one.'

Rafferty looked at Mr Alsop narrowly and he saw the man's face was serious.

'Just who are these friends of yours, Mr Alsop?' Rafferty asked cautiously.

'Well, it sounds funny,' Mr Alsop said, 'but I don't rightly know. They don't talk so very good. They don't talk at all. All we can get out of them is that their name is something about bending iron with a hammer.'

Rafferty had been circling the contraption, gradually drawing closer to it. He suddenly collided with something he couldn't see. He said 'ouch' and rubbed his shin.

'Oh, I forgot to tell you, Mr Rafferty,' Mr Alsop said, 'they got a gadget on it that won't let you get near, some kind of a wall you can't see. That's to keep boys away from it.'

'These friends of yours, Mr Alsop, where are they now?'

'Oh, they're over at the house,' Mr Alsop said. 'You can see them if you want to. But I think you'll find it pretty hard talking to them.'

'Russians?' Rafferty asked.

'Oh, no. I don't think so. They don't wear cossacks*.'

'Let's go,' Rafferty said in a low voice and led the way across the muddy barnyard toward the house.

'These folks come here the first time about six years ago,' Mr Alsop said. 'Wanted some eggs. Thought maybe they could raise chickens up where they are. Took 'em three years to get home. Eggs spoiled. So the folks turned right around and come back. This time I fixed 'em up a little brooder so they can raise chickens on the way home.' He suddenly laughed. 'I can just see that little contraption way out there in the sky full of chickens.'

Rafferty climbed up on the back porch ahead of Mr Alsop and went through the back door into the kitchen. Mr Alsop stopped him before they went into the living room.

'Now, Mr Rafferty, my wife can talk to these people better than I can, so anything you want to know you better ask her. Her and the lady get along pretty good.'

'Okay,' Rafferty said. He pushed Mr Alsop gently through the door into the living room, thinking he would play along, act naïve.

Mrs Alsop sat in an armchair close to a circulating heater. Rafferty saw the visitors sitting side by side on the davenport, he saw them waving their long, flexible antennae delicately, he saw their lavender faces as expressionless as glass, the round eyes that seemed to be painted on.

Rafferty clutched the door facings and stared.

Mrs Alsop turned toward him brightly.

'Mr Rafferty,' she said, 'these are the people that came to see us in that airplane.' Mrs Alsop raised her finger and both the strangers bent their antennae down in her direction.

'This is Mr Rafferty,' Mrs Alsop said. 'He's a newspaper reporter.

He wanted to see your airplane.'

Rafferty managed to nod and the strangers curled up their antennae and nodded politely. The woman scratched her side with her left claw.

Something inside Rafferty's head was saying, you're a smart boy, Rafferty, you're too smart to be taken in. Somebody's pulling a whopping, skilful publicity scheme, somebody's got you down for a sucker. Either that or you're crazy or drunk or dreaming.

Rafferty tried to keep his voice casual.

'What did you say their names are, Mrs Alsop?'

'Well, we don't know,' Mrs Alsop said. 'You see they can only make pictures for you. They point those funny squiggly horns at you and they just think. That makes you think, too – the same thing they're thinking. I asked them what their name is and then I let them think for me. All I saw was a picture of the man hammering some iron on an anvil. So I guess their name is something like Man-Who-Bends-Iron. Maybe it's kind of like an Indian* name.'

Rafferty looked slyly at the people who bent iron and at Mrs Alsop.

'Do you suppose,' he said innocently, 'they would talk to me – or *think* to me?'

Mrs Alsop looked troubled.

'They'd be glad to, Mr Rafferty. The only thing is, it's pretty hard at first. Hard for you, that is.'

'I'll try it,' Rafferty said. He took out a cigarette and lighted it. He held the match until it burned his fingers.

'Just throw it in the coal bucket,' Mr Alsop said.

Rafferty threw the match in the coal bucket.

'Ask these things . . . ah . . . people where they come from,' he said.

Mrs Alsop smiled. 'That's a very hard question. I asked them that before but I didn't get much of a picture. But I'll ask them again.'

Mrs Alsop raised her finger and both horns bent toward her and aimed directly at her head.

'This young man,' Mrs Alsop said in a loud voice like she was talking to someone hard of hearing, 'wants to know where you people come from.'

Mr Alsop nudged Rafferty. 'Just hold up your finger when you want your answer.'

Rafferty felt like a complete idiot but he held up his finger. The woman whose husband bends iron bent her antenna down until it focussed on Rafferty between the eyes. He involuntarily braced himself against the door facings. Suddenly his brain felt as though it were made of rubber and somebody was wringing and twisting and pounding it all out of shape and moulding it back together again into something new. The terror of it blinded him. He was flying through space, through a great white void. Stars and meteors whizzed by and a great star, dazzling with brilliance, white and sparkling stood there in his mind and then it went out. Rafferty's mind was released but he found himself trembling, clutching the door facings. His burning cigarette was on the floor. Mr Alsop stooped and picked it up.

'Here's your cigarette, Mr Rafferty. Did you get your answer?'

Rafferty was white.

'Mr Alsop!' he said. 'Mrs Alsop! This is on the level. These creatures are really from out there in space somewhere!'

Mr Alsop said: 'Sure, they come a long way.'

'Do you know what this means?' Rafferty heard his voice becoming hysterical and he tried to keep it calm. 'Do you know this is the most important thing that has ever happened in the history of the world? Do you know this is . . . yes, it is, it's the biggest story in the world and it's happening to me, do you understand?' Rafferty was yelling. 'Where's your phone?'

'We don't have a telephone,' Mr Alsop said. 'There's one down at the filling station. But these people are going to go in a few minutes. Why don't you wait and see them off? Already got their eggs and the brooder and feed on board.'

'No!' Rafferty gasped. 'They can't go in a few minutes! Listen, I've got to phone – I've got to get a photographer!'

Mrs Alsop smiled.

'Well, Mr Rafferty, we tried to get them to stay over for supper but they have to go at a certain time. They have to catch the tide or something like that.'

'It's the moon,' Mr Alsop said with authority. 'It's something about the moon being in the right place.'

The people from space sat there demurely, their claws folded in their laps, their antennae neatly curled to show they weren't eavesdropping on other people's minds.

Rafferty looked frantically around the room for a telephone he knew wasn't there. Got to get Joe Pegley at the city desk, Rafferty thought. Joe'll know what to do. No, no, Joe would say you're drunk.

But this is the biggest story in the world, Rafferty's brain kept saying. It's the biggest story in the world and you just stand here.

'Listen, Alsop!' Rafferty yelled. 'You got a camera? Any kind of a camera. I *got* to have a camera!'

'Oh, sure,' Mr Alsop said. 'I got a fine camera. It's a box camera but it takes good pictures. I'll show you some I took of my chickens.'

'No, no! I don't want to see your pictures. I want the camera!'

Mr Alsop went into the parlour and Rafferty could see him fumbling around on top of the organ.

'Mrs Alsop!' Rafferty shouted. 'I've got to ask lots of questions!'

'Ask away,' Mrs Alsop said cheerily. 'They don't mind.'

But what could you ask people from space? You got their names. You got what they were here for: eggs. You got where they were from . . .

Mr Alsop's voice came from the parlour.

'Ethel, you seen my camera?'

Mrs Alsop sighed. 'No, I haven't. You put it away.'

'Only trouble is,' Mr Alsop said, 'haven't got any films for it.'

Suddenly the people from space turned their antennae toward each other for a second and apparently coming to a mutual agreement, got up and darted here and there about the room as quick as fireflies, so fast Rafferty could scarcely see them. They scuttered out the door and off toward the barn. All Rafferty could think was: 'My God, they're part bug!'

Rafferty rushed out the door, on toward the barn through the mud, screaming at the creatures to stop. But before he was half-way there the gleaming plastic contraption slid out of the barn and there was a slight hiss. The thing disappeared into the low hanging clouds.

All there was left for Rafferty to see was a steaming place in the mud and a little circle of burnt earth. Rafferty sat down in the mud, a hollow, empty feeling in his middle, with the knowledge that the greatest story in the world had gone off into the sky. No pictures, no evidence, no story. He dully went over in his mind the information he had:

'Mr and Mrs Man-Who-Bends-Iron . . .' It slowly dawned on Rafferty what that meant. Smith! Man-Who-Bends-Iron on an anvil. Of course that was Smith*. . . 'Mr and Mrs Smith visited at the Alfred Alsop place Sunday. They returned to their home in the system of Alpha Centauri with two crates of hatching eggs.'

Rafferty got to his feet and shook his head. He stood still in the mud and suddenly his eyes narrowed and you knew that the Rafferty brain was working – that Rafferty brain that always came up with the story. He bolted for the house and burst in the back door.

'Alsop!' he yelled. 'Did those people pay you for those eggs?'

Mr Alsop was standing on a chair in front of the china closet, still hunting for the camera.

'Oh, sure,' he said. 'In a way they did.'

'Let me see the money!' Rafferty demanded.

'Oh, not in money,' Mr Alsop said. 'They don't have any money. But when they were here six years ago they brought us some eggs of their own in trade.'

'Six years ago!' Rafferty moaned. Then he started. 'Eggs! What kind of eggs?'

Mr Alsop chuckled a little. 'Oh, I don't know,' he said. 'We called them star ducks. The eggs were star shaped. And you know we set them under a hen and the star points bothered the old hen something awful.'

Mr Alsop climbed down from the chair.

'Star ducks aren't much good though. They look something like a little hippopotamus and something like a swallow. But they got six legs. Only two of them lived and we ate them for Thanksgiving.'

Rafferty's brain still worked, grasping for that single fragment of evidence that would make his city editor – and the world – believe.

Rafferty leaned closer. 'Mr Alsop,' he almost whispered, 'you wouldn't know where the skeletons of the star ducks are?'

Mr Alsop looked puzzled. 'You mean the bones? We gave the bones to the dog. That was five years ago. Even the dog's dead now.'

Rafferty picked up his hat like a man in a daze.

'Thanks, Mr Alsop,' he said dully. 'Thanks.'

Rafferty stood on the porch and put on his hat. He pushed it back on his head. He stared up into the overcast; he stared until he felt dizzy like he was spiralling off into the mist.

Mr Alsop came out, wiping the dust off a box camera with his sleeve.

'Oh, Mr Rafferty,' he said. 'I found the camera.'

NOTES

Yankee (p25)

   (sometimes derogatory) an inhabitant of any of the northern American
   States, especially those of New England

thirty-six point Bodoni (p27)

   the size (very large) and name of a printer's typeface

cossacks (p28)

   a section of the Russian population (Mr Alsop is probably confusing
   the word with *cassock*, a long black garment worn by some priests)

Indian (p29)

   American Indian (the preferred term now is Native American); the
   original inhabitants of North America, whose names are often descriptive
   of the natural world (e.g. Sitting Bull, Laughing Water)

Smith (p32)

   one of the most ordinary and widespread family names among English-
   speaking peoples; it originally meant a blacksmith, a person who made
   and repaired things made of iron, especially horseshoes

DISCUSSION

1   What is Rafferty's attitude to the Alsops, and what is his first thought
    after Mrs Man-Who-Bends-Iron tries to implant some information in
    his mind? What do his reactions reveal about his character?

2   How do the Alsops behave to their visitors from outer space? Do you
    find their approach refreshing, or exasperating, in that a great
    opportunity is being missed?

3   Do you feel sympathy for Rafferty in his predicament? Might he have
    got evidence for his news story if he himself had behaved differently?
    Suggest how he might have dealt with the situation in a better way.

4   Did you find this story amusing? Why, or why not? Is the author using
    humour to make a critical point about news reporting in general? If so,
    do you agree with the implied criticism?

LANGUAGE FOCUS

1   Find these expressions in the text of the story and then rephrase them
    in your own words.

mentally pegging him a taciturn Yankee (p25)
I guess it was a phony tip (p26)
for sheer dumbness, these Alsops had them all beat (p26)
you're too smart to be taken in (p29)
Somebody's got you down for a sucker (p29)
This is on the level (p30)
that Rafferty brain that always came up with the story (p32)
the star points bothered the old hen something awful (p33)

2   The visitors from outer space are referred to by the following terms in
the story. Without looking back at the text, can you say which terms
are used by Rafferty, and which by the Alsops? What do the terms
suggest about the attitudes of the speakers?

folks, friends, Russians, people, things, creatures, part bug

Which adjectives from the following list might describe the attitudes
of the Alsops and Rafferty? Explain the reasons for your choice.

*dismissive, courteous, naive, patronizing, amiable, contemptuous,
unsophisticated, insensitive, hostile, perceptive, incurious, hospitable,
self-important, well-meaning, stupid, worldly-wise*

ACTIVITIES

1   Imagine what the visitors from space might have been saying to each
other just before they hurried back to their spacecraft. What effect
might Rafferty's shouting and excitable behaviour have had on them?
Write down a possible conversation between the 'Smiths'.

2   Rafferty decides to write a report for his newspaper anyway. Think of
a suitable headline and write his report for him. News reports are not
always very accurate or truthful. What embellishments could you add
to the few basic facts, to try and convince the reading public that the
story was a true one and not a hoax?

3   Rafferty can only think of three questions to ask the visitors. What
questions would have occurred to you in that situation? Devise ten
questions that would obtain the maximum amount of information,
in case the visitors return in six years' time for some more eggs.

HUMAN IS

THE AUTHOR

Philip K. Dick was born in Chicago in 1928, and spent most of his life in California. He attended college for one year at Berkeley, and at one time ran a record shop and also a classical music programme for a local radio station. His science-fiction writing is brilliantly inventive, often exploring the unreliability of perception and different 'levels of reality' created by hallucinogenic drugs and schizophrenic delusion. His best-known works include *The Man in the High Castle* (an award-winning novel of alternative history), *Martian Time-Slip, Dr Bloodmoney, The Three Stigmata of Palmer Eldritch*, and *Do Androids Dream of Electric Sheep?*, which was filmed as *Blade Runner*. He died in 1982.

THE STORY

What does it mean to be 'human'? Beyond the obvious biological description, the definition can be hard to pin down, depending on one's individual beliefs. Do human beings have souls? What *is* a soul? Are we different from other life-forms because of our capacity to feel emotions, such as compassion and kindness and grief? Or because we are capable of being cruel, sadistic . . . and *in*human?

Jill Herrick lives in an age when the human race has extended its dominance to other planets, and over alien life-forms. Technology has the answer to all of life's difficulties – except the human ones. An unhappy marriage is still an unhappy marriage. Jill's eyes fill with tears as she listens to her husband's cold, ruthless voice . . .

HUMAN IS

Jill Herrick's blue eyes filled with tears. She gazed at her husband in unspeakable horror. 'You're – you're hideous!' she wailed.

Lester Herrick continued working, arranging heaps of notes and graphs in precise piles.

'Hideous,' he stated, 'is a value judgment. It contains no factual information.' He sent a report tape on Centauran parasitic life whizzing through the desk scanner. 'Merely an opinion. An expression of emotion, nothing more.'

Jill stumbled back to the kitchen. Listlessly, she waved her hand to trip the stove into activity. Conveyor belts in the wall hummed to life, hurrying the food from the underground storage lockers for the evening meal.

She turned to face her husband one last time. 'Not even a *little* while?' she begged. 'Not even—'

'Not even for a month. When he comes you can tell him. If you haven't the courage, I'll do it. I can't have a child running around here. I have too much work to do. This report on Betelgeuse XI is due in ten days.' Lester dropped a spool on Fomalhautan fossil implements into the scanner. 'What's the matter with your brother? Why can't he take care of his own child?'

Jill dabbed at swollen eyes. 'Don't you understand? I *want* Gus here! I begged Frank to let him come. And now you—'

'I'll be glad when he's old enough to be turned over to the Government.' Lester's thin face twisted in annoyance. 'Damn it, Jill, isn't dinner ready yet? It's been ten minutes! What's wrong with that stove?'

'It's almost ready.' The stove showed a red signal light. The robant waiter had come out of the wall and was waiting expectantly to take the food.

Jill sat down and blew her small nose violently. In the living-room, Lester worked on unperturbed. His work. His research. Day after day. Lester was getting ahead; there was no doubt of that. His lean body was bent like a coiled spring over the tape scanner, cold gray eyes taking in the information feverishly, analyzing, appraising, his conceptual faculties operating like well-greased machinery.

Jill's lips trembled in misery and resentment. Gus – little Gus. How could she tell him? Fresh tears welled up in her eyes. Never to see the chubby little fellow again. He could never come back – because his childish laughter and play bothered Lester. Interfered with his research.

The stove clicked to green. The food slid out, into the arms of the robant. Soft chimes sounded to announce dinner.

'I hear it,' Lester grated. He snapped off the scanner and got to his feet. 'I suppose he'll come while we're eating.'

'I can vid* Frank and ask—'

'No. Might as well get it over with.' Lester nodded impatiently to the robant. 'All right. Put it down.' His thin lips set in an angry line. 'Damn it, don't dawdle! I want to get back to my work!'

Jill bit back the tears.

Little Gus came trailing into the house as they were finishing dinner.

Jill gave a cry of joy. 'Gussie!' She ran to sweep him up in her arms. 'I'm so glad to see you!'

'Watch out for my tiger,' Gus muttered. He dropped his little gray kitten onto the rug and it rushed off, under the couch. 'He's hiding.'

Lester's eyes flickered as he studied the little boy and the tip of gray tail extending from under the couch.

'Why do you call it a tiger? It's nothing but an alley cat.'

Gus looked hurt. He scowled. 'He's a tiger. He's got stripes.'

'Tigers are yellow and a great deal bigger. You might as well learn to classify things by their correct names.'

'Lester, please—' Jill pleaded.

'Be quiet,' her husband said crossly. 'Gus is old enough to shed childish illusions and develop a realistic orientation. What's wrong with the psych* testers? Don't they straighten this sort of nonsense out?'

Gus ran and snatched up his tiger. 'You leave him alone!'

Lester contemplated the kitten. A strange, cold smile played about his lips. 'Come down to the lab some time, Gus. We'll show you lots of cats. We use them in our research. Cats, guinea pigs, rabbits—'

'Lester!' Jill gasped. 'How can you!'

Lester laughed thinly. Abruptly he broke off and returned to his desk. 'Now clear out of here. I have to finish these reports. And don't forget to tell Gus.'

Gus got excited. 'Tell me what?' His cheeks flushed. His eyes sparkled. 'What is it? Something for me? A *secret*?'

Jill's heart was like lead. She put her hand heavily on the child's shoulder. 'Come on, Gus. We'll go sit out in the garden and I'll tell you. Bring – bring your tiger.'

A click. The emergency vidsender lit up. Instantly Lester was on his feet. 'Be quiet!' He ran to the sender, breathing rapidly. 'Nobody speak!'

Jill and Gus paused at the door. A confidential message was sliding from the slot into the dish. Lester grabbed it up and broke the seal. He studied it intently.

'What is it?' Jill asked. 'Anything bad?'

'Bad?' Lester's face shone with a deep inner glow. 'No, not bad at all.' He glanced at his watch. 'Just time. Let's see, I'll need—'

'What is it?'

'I'm going on a trip. I'll be gone two or three weeks. Rexor IV is into the charted area.'

'Rexor IV? You're going there?' Jill clasped her hands eagerly.

'Oh, I've always wanted to see an old system, old ruins and cities! Lester, can I come along? Can I go with you? We never took a vacation, and you always promised . . .'

Lester Herrick stared at his wife in amazement. 'You?' he said. '*You* go along?' He laughed unpleasantly. 'Now hurry and get my things together. I've been waiting for this a long time.' He rubbed his hands together in satisfaction. 'You can keep the boy here until I'm back. But no longer. Rexor IV! I can hardly wait!'

'You have to make allowances,' Frank said. 'After all, he's a scientist.'

'I don't care,' Jill said. 'I'm leaving him. As soon as he gets back from Rexor IV. I've made up my mind.'

Her brother was silent, deep in thought. He stretched his feet out, onto the lawn of the little garden. 'Well, if you leave him you'll be free to marry again. You're still classed as sexually adequate, aren't you?'

Jill nodded firmly. 'You bet I am. I wouldn't have any trouble. Maybe I can find somebody who likes children.'

'You think a lot of children,' Frank perceived. 'Gus loves to visit you. But he doesn't like Lester. Les needles him.'

'I know. This past week has been heaven, with him gone.' Jill patted her soft blonde hair, blushing prettily. 'I've had fun. Makes me feel alive again.'

'When'll he be back?'

'Any day.' Jill clenched her small fists. 'We've been married five years and every year it's worse. He's so – so inhuman. Utterly cold and ruthless. Him and his work. Day and night.'

'Les is ambitious. He wants to get to the top in his field.' Frank lit a cigarette lazily. 'A pusher. Well, maybe he'll do it. What's he in?'

'Toxicology. He works out new poisons for Military. He invented the copper sulphate skin-lime they used against Callisto.'

'It's a small field. Now take me.' Frank leaned contentedly against the wall of the house. 'There are thousands of Clearance lawyers. I could work for years and never create a ripple. I'm content just to be. I do my job. I enjoy it.'

'I wish Lester felt that way.'

'Maybe he'll change.'

'He'll *never* change,' Jill said bitterly. 'I know that, now. That's why I've made up my mind to leave him. He'll always be the same.'

Lester Herrick came back from Rexor IV a different man. Beaming happily, he deposited his anti-grav* suitcase in the arms of the waiting robant. 'Thank you.'

Jill gasped speechlessly. 'Les! What—'

Lester removed his hat, bowing a little. 'Good day, my dear. You're looking lovely. Your eyes are clear and blue. Sparkling like some virgin lake, fed by mountain streams.' He sniffed. 'Do I smell a delicious repast warming on the hearth?'

'Oh, Lester.' Jill blinked uncertainly, faint hope swelling in her bosom. 'Lester, what's happened to you? You're so – so different.'

'Am I, my dear?' Lester moved about the house, touching things and sighing. 'What a dear little house. So sweet and friendly. You don't know how wonderful it is to be here. Believe me.'

'I'm afraid to believe it,' Jill said.

'Believe what?'

'That you mean all this. That you're not the way you were. The way you've always been.'

'What way is that?'

'Mean. Mean and cruel.'

'I?' Lester frowned, rubbing his lip. 'Hmm. Interesting.' He brightened. 'Well, that's all in the past. What's for dinner? I'm faint with hunger.'

Jill eyed him uncertainly as she moved into the kitchen. 'Anything you want, Lester. You know our stove covers the maximum select-list.'

'Of course.' Lester coughed rapidly. 'Well, shall we try sirloin steak, medium, smothered in onions? With mushroom sauce. And white rolls. With hot coffee. Perhaps ice cream and apple pie for dessert.'

'You never seemed to care much about food,' Jill said thoughtfully.

'Oh?'

'You always said you hoped eventually they'd make intravenous intake universally applicable.' She studied her husband intently. 'Lester, what's happened?'

'Nothing. Nothing at all.' Lester carelessly took his pipe out and lit it rapidly, somewhat awkwardly. Bits of tobacco drifted to the rug. He bent nervously down and tried to pick them up again. 'Please go about your tasks and don't mind me. Perhaps I can help you prepare – that is, can I do anything to help?'

'No,' Jill said. 'I can do it. You go ahead with your work, if you want.'

'Work?'

'Your research. In toxins.'

'Toxins!' Lester showed confusion. 'Well, for heaven's sake! Toxins. Devil take it!'

'What, dear?'

'I mean, I really feel too tired, just now. I'll work later.' Lester moved vaguely around the room. 'I think I'll sit and enjoy being home again. Off that awful Rexor IV.'

'Was it awful?'

'Horrible.' A spasm of disgust crossed Lester's face. 'Dry and dead. Ancient. Squeezed to a pulp by wind and sun. A dreadful place, my dear.'

'I'm sorry to hear that. I always wanted to visit it.'

'Heaven forbid!' Lester cried feelingly. 'You stay right here, my dear. With me. The – the two of us.' His eyes wandered around the room. 'Two, yes. Terra is a wonderful planet. Moist and full of life.' He beamed happily. 'Just right.'

'I don't understand it,' Jill said.

'Repeat all the things you remember,' Frank said. His robot pencil poised itself alertly. 'The changes you've noticed in him. I'm curious.'

'Why?'

'No reason. Go on. You say you sensed it right away? That he was different?'

'I noticed it at once. The expression on his face. Not that hard, practical look. A sort of mellow look. Relaxed. Tolerant. A sort of calmness.'

'I see,' Frank said. 'What else?'

Jill peered nervously through the back door into the house. 'He can't hear us, can he?'

'No. He's inside playing with Gus. In the living-room. They're Venusian otter-men today. Your husband built an otter slide down at his lab. I saw him unwrapping it.'

'His talk.'

'His what?'

'The way he talks. His choice of words. Words he never used before. Whole new phrases. Metaphors. I never heard him use a metaphor in all our five years together. He said metaphors were inexact. Misleading. And—'

'And what?' The pencil scratched busily.

'And they're *strange* words. Old words. Words you don't hear any more.'

'Archaic phraseology?' Frank asked tensely.

'Yes.' Jill paced back and forth across the small lawn, her hands in the pockets of her plastic shorts. 'Formal words. Like something—'

'Something out of a book?'

'Exactly! You've noticed it?'

'I noticed it.' Frank's face was grim. 'Go on.'

Jill stopped pacing. 'What's on your mind? Do you have a theory?'

'I want to know more facts.'

She reflected. 'He plays. With Gus. He plays and jokes. And he – he eats.'

'Didn't he eat before?'

'Not like he does now. Now he *loves* food. He goes into the kitchen and tries endless combinations. He and the stove get together and cook up all sorts of weird things.'

'I thought he'd put on weight.'

'He's gained ten pounds. He eats, smiles and laughs. He's constantly polite.' Jill glanced away coyly. 'He's even – romantic! He always said *that* was irrational. And he's not interested in his work. His research in toxins.'

'I see.' Frank chewed his lip. 'Anything more?'

'One thing puzzles me very much. I've noticed it again and again.'

'What is it?'

'He seems to have strange lapses of—'

A burst of laughter. Lester Herrick, eyes bright with merriment, came rushing out of the house, little Gus close behind.

'We have an announcement!' Lester cried.

'An announzelmen,' Gus echoed.

Frank folded his notes up and slid them into his coat pocket. The pencil hurried after them. He got slowly to his feet. 'What is it?'

'You make it,' Lester said, taking little Gus's hand and leading him forward.

Gus's plump face screwed up in concentration. 'I'm going to come live with you,' he stated. Anxiously he watched Jill's expression. 'Lester says I can. Can I? Can I, Aunt Jill?'

Her heart flooded with incredible joy. She glanced from Gus to Lester. 'Do you – do you really mean it?' Her voice was almost inaudible.

Lester put his arm around her, holding her close to him. 'Of course, we mean it,' he said gently. His eyes were warm and understanding. 'We wouldn't tease you, my dear.'

'No teasing!' Gus shouted excitedly. 'No more teasing!' He and Lester and Jill drew close together. 'Never again!'

Frank stood a little way off, his face grim. Jill noticed him and broke away abruptly. 'What is it?' she faltered. 'Is anything—'

'When you're quite finished,' Frank said to Lester Herrick, 'I'd like you to come with me.'

A chill clutched Jill's heart. 'What is it? Can I come, too?'

Frank shook his head. He moved toward Lester ominously. 'Come on, Herrick. Let's go. You and I are going to take a little trip.'

The three Federal Clearance Agents took up positions a few feet from Lester Herrick, vibro-tubes gripped alertly.

Clearance Director Douglas studied Herrick for a long time. 'You're sure?' he said finally.

'Absolutely,' Frank stated.

'When did he get back from Rexor IV?'

'A week ago.'

'And the change was noticeable at once?'

'His wife noticed it as soon as she saw him. There's no doubt it occurred on Rexor.' Frank paused significantly. 'And you know what that means.'

'I know.' Douglas walked slowly around the seated man, examining him from every angle.

Lester Herrick sat quietly, his coat neatly folded across his knee. He rested his hands on his ivory-topped cane, his face calm and expressionless. He wore a soft gray suit, a subdued necktie, French cuffs, and shiny black shoes. He said nothing.

'Their methods are simple and exact,' Douglas said. 'The original psychic contents are removed and stored – in some sort of suspension. The interjection of the substitute contents is instantaneous. Lester Herrick was probably poking around the Rexor city ruins, ignoring the safety precautions – shield or manual screen – and they got him.'

The seated man stirred. 'I'd like very much to communicate with Jill,' he murmured. 'She surely is becoming anxious.'

Frank turned away, face choked with revulsion. 'God. It's still pretending.'

Director Douglas restrained himself with the greatest effort. 'It's certainly an amazing thing. No physical changes. You could look at it and never know.' He moved toward the seated man, his face hard. 'Listen to me, whatever you call yourself. Can you understand what I say?'

'Of course,' Lester Herrick answered.

'Did you really think you'd get away with it? We caught the others – the ones before you. All ten of them. Even before they got here.' Douglas grinned coldly. 'Vibro-rayed them one after another.'

The color left Lester Herrick's face. Sweat came out on his forehead. He wiped it away with a silk handkerchief from his breast pocket. 'Oh?' he murmured.

'You're not fooling us. All Terra is alerted for you Rexorians. I'm surprised you got off Rexor at all. Herrick must have been extremely careless. We stopped the others aboard ship. Fried them out in deep space.'

'Herrick had a private ship,' the seated man murmured. 'He bypassed the check station going in. No record of his arrival existed. He was never checked.'

'*Fry it!*' Douglas grated. The three Clearance agents lifted their tubes, moving forward.

'No.' Frank shook his head. 'We can't. It's a bad situation.'

'What do you mean? Why can't we? We fried the others—'

'They were caught in deep space. This is Terra. Terran law, not military law, applies.' Frank waved toward the seated man. 'And it's in a human body. It comes under regular civil laws. We've got to *prove* it's not Lester Herrick – that it's a Rexorian infiltrator. It's going to be tough. But it can be done.'

'How?'

'His wife. Herrick's wife. Her testimony. Jill Herrick can assert the difference between Lester Herrick and this thing. She knows – and I think we can make it stand up in court.'

It was late afternoon. Frank drove his surface cruiser slowly along. Neither he nor Jill spoke.

'So that's it,' Jill said at last. Her face was gray. Her eyes dry and bright, without emotion. 'I knew it was too good to be true.' She tried to smile. 'It seemed so wonderful.'

'I know,' Frank said. 'It's a terrible damn thing. If only—'

'*Why?*' Jill said. 'Why did he – did it do this? Why did it take Lester's body?'

'Rexor IV is old. Dead. A dying planet. Life is dying out.'

'I remember, now. He – it said something like that. Something about Rexor. That it was glad to get away.'

'The Rexorians are an old race. The few that remain are feeble. They've been trying to migrate for centuries. But their bodies are too weak. Some tried to migrate to Venus – and died instantly. They worked out this system about a century ago.'

'But it knows so much. About us. It speaks our language.'

'Not quite. The changes you mentioned. The odd diction. You see, the Rexorians have only a vague knowledge of human beings. A sort of ideal abstraction, taken from Terran objects that have found their way to Rexor. Books mostly. Secondary data like that. The Rexorian idea of Terra is based on centuries-old Terran literature. Romantic novels from our past. Language, customs, manners from old Terran books.

'That accounts for the strange archaic quality to *it*. It had studied Terra, all right. But in an indirect and misleading way.' Frank grinned wryly. 'The Rexorians are two hundred years behind the times – which is a break for us. That's how we're able to detect them.'

'Is this sort of thing – common? Does it happen often? It seems unbelievable.' Jill rubbed her forehead wearily. 'Dreamlike. It's hard to realize that it's actually happened. I'm just beginning to understand what it means.'

'The galaxy is full of alien life forms. Parasitic and destructive entities. Terran ethics don't extend to them. We have to guard constantly against this sort of thing. Lester went in unsuspectingly – and this thing ousted him and took over his body.'

Frank glanced at his sister. Jill's face was expressionless. A stern little face, wide-eyed, but composed. She sat up straight, staring fixedly ahead, her small hands folded quietly in her lap.

'We can arrange it so you won't actually have to appear in court,' Frank went on. 'You can vid a statement and it'll be presented as evidence. I'm certain your statement will do. The Federal courts will help us all they can, but they have to have *some* evidence to go on.'

Jill was silent.

'What do you say?' Frank asked.

'What happens after the court makes its decision?'

'Then we vibro-ray it. Destroy the Rexorian mind. A Terran patrol ship on Rexor IV sends out a party to locate the – er – original contents.'

Jill gasped. She turned toward her brother in amazement. 'You mean—'

'Oh, yes. Lester is alive. In suspension, somewhere on Rexor. In one of the old city ruins. We'll have to force them to give him up. They won't want to, but they'll do it. They've done it before. Then he'll be back with you. Safe and sound. Just like before. And this horrible nightmare you've been living will be a thing of the past.'

'I see.'

'Here we are.' The cruiser pulled to a halt before the imposing Federal Clearance Building. Frank got quickly out, holding the door for his sister. Jill stepped down slowly. 'Okay?' Frank said.

'Okay.'

When they entered the building, Clearance agents led them through the check screens, down the long corridors. Jill's high heels echoed in the ominous silence.

'Quite a place,' Frank observed.

'It's unfriendly.'

'Consider it a glorified police station.' Frank halted. Before them was a guarded door. 'Here we are.'

'Wait.' Jill pulled back, her face twisting in panic. 'I—'

'We'll wait until you're ready.' Frank signaled to the Clearance agent to leave. 'I understand. It's a bad business.'

Jill stood for a moment, her head down. She took a deep breath, her small fists clenched. Her chin came up, level and steady. 'All right.'

'You ready?'

'Yes.'

Frank opened the door. 'Here we are.'

Director Douglas and the three Clearance agents turned expectantly as Jill and Frank entered. 'Good,' Douglas murmured, with relief. 'I was beginning to get worried.'

The sitting man got slowly to his feet, picking up his coat. He gripped his ivory-headed cane tightly, his hands tense. He said nothing. He watched silently as the woman entered the room, Frank behind her. 'This is Mrs Herrick,' Frank said. 'Jill, this is Clearance Director Douglas.'

'I've heard of you,' Jill said faintly.

'Then you know our work.'

'Yes. I know your work.'

'This is an unfortunate business. It's happened before. I don't know what Frank has told you . . .'

'He explained the situation.'

'Good.' Douglas was relieved. 'I'm glad of that. It's not easy to explain. You understand, then, what we want. The previous cases were caught in deep space. We vibro-tubed them and got the original contents back. But this time we must work through legal channels.' Douglas picked up a vidtape recorder. 'We will need your statement, Mrs Herrick. Since no physical change has occurred we'll have no direct evidence to make our case. We'll have only your testimony of character alteration to present to the court.'

He held the vidtape recorder out. Jill took it slowly.

'Your statement will undoubtedly be accepted by the court. The court will give us the release we want and then we can go ahead. If everything goes correctly we hope to be able to set things exactly as they were before.'

Jill was gazing silently at the man standing in the corner with his coat and ivory-headed cane. 'Before?' she said. 'What do you mean?'

'Before the change.'

Jill turned toward Director Douglas. Calmly, she laid the vidtape recorder down on the table. 'What change are you talking about?'

Douglas paled. He licked his lips. All eyes in the room were on Jill. 'The change in *him*.' He pointed at the man.

'Jill!' Frank barked. 'What's the matter with you?' He came quickly toward her. 'What the hell are you doing? You know damn well what change we mean!'

'That's odd,' Jill said thoughtfully. 'I haven't noticed any change.'

Frank and Director Douglas looked at each other. 'I don't get it,' Frank muttered, dazed.

'Mrs Herrick—' Douglas began.

Jill walked over to the man standing quietly in the corner. 'Can we go now, dear?' she asked. She took his arm. 'Or is there some reason why my husband has to stay here?'

The man and woman walked silently along the dark street.

'Come on,' Jill said. 'Let's go home.'

The man glanced at her. 'It's a nice afternoon,' he said. He took a deep breath, filling his lungs. 'Spring is coming – I think. Isn't it?'

Jill nodded.

'I wasn't sure. It's a nice smell. Plants and soil and growing things.'

'Yes.'

'Are we going to walk? Is it far?'

'Not too far.'

The man gazed at her intently, a serious expression on his face. 'I am very indebted to you, my dear,' he said.

Jill nodded.

'I wish to thank you. I must admit I did not expect such a—'

Jill turned abruptly. 'What is your name? Your *real* name.'

The man's gray eyes flickered. He smiled a little, a kind, gentle smile. 'I'm afraid you would not be able to pronounce it. The sounds cannot be formed . . .'

Jill was silent as they walked along, deep in thought. The city lights were coming on all around them. Bright yellow spots in the gloom. 'What are you thinking?' the man asked.

'I was thinking perhaps I will still call you Lester,' Jill said. 'If you don't mind.'

'I don't mind,' the man said. He put his arm around her, drawing her close to him. He gazed down tenderly as they walked through the thickening darkness, between the yellow candles of light that marked the way. 'Anything you wish. Whatever will make you happy.'

NOTES

vid (p38)

> an invented word, probably short for something like 'videosend' or 'videocall', i.e. to send or call by video

pysch testers (p39)

> the author's abbreviation for 'psychology testers'

anti-grav (p41)

> the author's abbreviation for 'anti-gravity', a hypothetical force opposing gravity

DISCUSSION

1 At what point in the story do you think Jill privately decides to accept the Rexorian Lester? Why does she make that decision? Do you sympathize with it? Why, or why not?

2 Do you find the idea of replacing a person's 'psychic contents' an alarming one? If it ever became technically possible to give new personalities to people, should it be a voluntary process, or obligatory for certain kinds of people? What kinds of people might be chosen? Make a list of possible candidates. Do you think this would be a useful or desirable step for society to take? Why, or why not?

3 In later years, Philip K. Dick wrote a note about this story:

> To me, this story states my early conclusions as to what is human. [...] It's not what you look like, or what planet you were born on. It's how kind you are. The quality of kindness, to me, distinguishes us from rocks and sticks and metal, and will forever, whatever shape we take, wherever we go, whatever we become.

Do you agree with the author's definition? What other characteristics could be said to be uniquely human?

LANGUAGE FOCUS

1 As well as the items in the Notes, the following invented words are used in the text. Try to guess, from the context of the story, what these futuristic inventions are, and what their purpose is. Can you suggest what existing words these new ones might be derived from?

> *robant* (p37)   *vidsender* (p39)   *vibro-tubes* (p45)   *vibro-ray* (p46)

2   Rephrase these expressions from the story in your own words.

> *Might as well get it over with.* (p38)
> *Jill's heart was like lead.* (p39)
> *Les needles him.* (p40)
> *This past week has been heaven.* (p40)
> *and never create a ripple* (p41)
> *Squeezed to a pulp by wind and sun.* (p42)
> *I think we can make it stand up in court.* (p47)
> *which is a break for us* (p48)

3   The following adjectives, taken from adjectives and adverbs in the story, can all describe human characteristics and emotions. Divide them into two groups, according to whether you think they have positive or negative connotations. Use a dictionary if necessary. How many of them could have a positive or a negative meaning, depending on the context in which they were used?

> *ambitious, bitter, calm, careless, cold, content, cruel, excited, gentle, grim, hard, impatient, inhuman, irrational, kind, lazy, mean, mellow, nervous, polite, practical, relaxed, romantic, ruthless, stern, thoughtful, tolerant, understanding, warm.*

4   The title *Human Is [as human does]* echoes the proverb, 'Handsome is as handsome does', which means that it's not what you look like that is important, but what you do. Why do you think the author gave the story this title? What title would you have chosen?

ACTIVITIES

1   What might the Rexorian Lester be thinking as he escapes from Rexor IV to Terra? Write his diary for the day he arrives at Jill's house.

2   After her decision to accept the 'new' Lester, Jill might be rather worried about her brother's reaction, because of the evidence she initially gave him. Imagine you are Jill and write a letter to Frank, explaining the change in Lester as convincingly as you can. Invent plausible explanations for his old-fashioned language, his lapses of memory, his newly romantic attitude, and so on.

3   There are glimpses in the story of what Terran society is like. For example, when Gus is old enough, he will be 'turned over to the government'. What do you imagine that might mean? Invent a short description of Terran society and ethics, using the clues you can find in the text. Then compare your notes with those of other students.

It's a Good Life

The Author

Jerome Bixby was born in the USA in 1923. He was a prolific story-writer, though relatively little of his work is science fiction. His stories include many Westerns, and he has also written science-fiction and horror screenplays and television plays, including several episodes of the series *Star Trek*. One of his novels, *Day of the Dove*, was based on this series. Volumes of his short stories are *Space by the Tale* and *Devil's Scrapbook*. His best-known and widely anthologized story, *It's a Good Life*, is a combination of science fiction and horror.

The Story

The English poet John Dryden wrote:
Of all the tyrannies on humankind,
The worst is that which persecutes the mind.
Science fiction often presents us with novel forms of tyranny, showing the human race subjugated by aliens or machines or cosmic forces, but the most terrifying tyrant must surely be the one who has telepathic powers, who can see into every corner of your mind, read your every thought, anticipate your every move.

The little village of Peaksville lives under a reign of terror, a random, unpredictable malevolence from which there is no escape. You must be very careful, very, very careful, all the time – even when doing something as harmless as delivering the groceries to the Fremont house, where little Anthony sits playing on the lawn . . .

It's a Good Life

A unt Amy was out on the front porch, rocking back and forth in the highbacked chair and fanning herself, when Bill Soames rode his bicycle up the road and stopped in front of the house.

Perspiring under the afternoon 'sun', Bill lifted the box of groceries out of the big basket over the front wheel of the bike, and came up the front walk.

Little Anthony was sitting on the lawn, playing with a rat. He had caught the rat down in the basement – he had made it think that it smelled cheese, the most rich-smelling and crumbly-delicious cheese a rat had ever thought it smelled, and it had come out of its hole, and now Anthony had hold of it with his mind and was making it do tricks.

When the rat saw Bill Soames coming, it tried to run, but Anthony thought at it, and it turned a flip-flop on the grass, and lay trembling, its eyes gleaming in small black terror.

Bill Soames hurried past Anthony and reached the front steps, mumbling. He always mumbled when he came to the Fremont house, or passed by it, or even thought of it. Everybody did. They thought about silly things, things that didn't mean very much, like two-and-two-is-four-and-twice-is-eight and so on; they tried to jumble up their thoughts and keep them skipping back and forth, so Anthony couldn't read their minds. The mumbling helped. Because if Anthony got anything strong out of your thoughts, he might take a notion to do something about it – like curing your wife's sick headaches or your kid's mumps, or getting your old milk cow back on schedule, or fixing the privy. And while Anthony mightn't actually mean any harm, he couldn't be expected to have much notion of what was the right thing to do in such cases.

That was if he liked you. He might try to help you, in his way.

And that could be pretty horrible.

If he didn't like you . . . well, that could be worse.

Bill Soames set the box of groceries on the porch railing, and stopped his mumbling long enough to say, 'Everythin' you wanted, Miss Amy.'

'Oh, fine, William,' Amy Fremont said lightly. 'My, ain't it terrible hot today?'

Bill Soames almost cringed. His eyes pleaded with her. He shook his head violently *no*, and then interrupted his mumbling again, though obviously he didn't want to: 'Oh, don't say that, Miss Amy . . . it's fine, just fine. A real *good* day!'

Amy Fremont got up from the rocking chair, and came across the porch. She was a tall woman, thin, a smiling vacancy in her eyes. About a year ago, Anthony had gotten mad at her, because she'd told him he shouldn't have turned the cat into a cat-rug, and although he had always obeyed her more than anyone else, which was hardly at all, this time he'd snapped at her. With his mind. And that had been the end of Amy Fremont's bright eyes, and the end of Amy Fremont as everyone had known her. And that was when word got around in Peaksville (population: 46) that even the members of Anthony's own family weren't safe. After that, everyone was twice as careful.

Someday Anthony might undo what he'd done to Aunt Amy. Anthony's Mom and Pop hoped he would. When he was older, and maybe sorry. If it was possible, that is. Because Aunt Amy had changed a lot, and besides, now Anthony wouldn't obey anyone.

'Land alive*, William,' Aunt Amy said, 'you don't have to mumble like that. Anthony wouldn't hurt you. My goodness, Anthony likes you!' She raised her voice and called to Anthony, who had tired of the rat and was making it eat itself. 'Don't you, dear? Don't you like Mr Soames?'

Anthony looked across the lawn at the grocery man – a bright, wet, purple gaze. He didn't say anything. Bill Soames tried to smile at him. After a second Anthony returned his attention to the rat. It had already devoured its tail, or at least chewed it off – for Anthony had made it bite faster than it could swallow, and little pink and red furry pieces lay around it on the green grass. Now the rat was having trouble reaching its hindquarters.

Mumbling silently, thinking of nothing in particular as hard as he could, Bill Soames went stiff-legged down the walk, mounted his bicycle and pedalled off.

'We'll see you tonight, William,' Aunt Amy called after him.

As Bill Soames pumped the pedals, he was wishing deep down that he could pump twice as fast, to get away from Anthony all the faster, and away from Aunt Amy, who sometimes just forgot how *careful* you had to be. And he shouldn't have thought that. Because Anthony caught it. He caught the desire to get away from the Fremont house as if it was something *bad*, and his purple gaze blinked, and he snapped a small, sulky thought after Bill Soames – just a small one, because he was in a good mood today, and besides, he liked Bill Soames, or at least didn't dislike him, at least today. Bill Soames wanted to go away – so, petulantly, Anthony helped him.

Pedalling with superhuman speed – or rather, appearing to, because in reality the bicycle was pedalling *him* – Bill Soames vanished down the road in a cloud of dust, his thin, terrified wail drifting back across the summerlike heat.

Anthony looked at the rat. It had devoured half its belly, and had died from pain. He thought it into a grave out deep in the cornfield – his father had once said, smiling, that he might as well do that with the things he killed – and went around the house, casting his odd shadow in the hot, brassy light from above.

In the kitchen, Aunt Amy was unpacking the groceries. She put the Mason-jarred goods on the shelves, and the meat and milk in the icebox, and the beet sugar and coarse flour in big cans under the sink. She put the cardboard box in the corner, by the door, for Mr Soames to pick up next time he came. It was stained and battered and torn and worn fuzzy, but it was one of the few left in Peaksville. In faded red letters it said *Campbell's Soup*. The last cans of soup, or of anything else, had been eaten long ago, except for a small communal hoard which the villagers dipped into for special occasions – but the box lingered on, like a coffin, and when it and the other boxes were gone, the men would have to make some out of wood.

Aunt Amy went out in back, where Anthony's Mom – Aunt Amy's sister – sat in the shade of the house, shelling peas. The peas, every time Mom ran a finger along a pod, went *lollop-lollop-lollop* into the pan on her lap.

'William brought the groceries,' Aunt Amy said. She sat down wearily in the straightbacked chair beside Mom, and began fanning herself again. She wasn't really old; but ever since Anthony had snapped at her with his mind, something had seemed to be wrong with her body as well as her mind, and she was tired all the time.

'Oh, good,' said Mom. *Lollop* went the fat peas into the pan.

Everybody in Peaksville always said 'Oh, fine,' or 'Good,' or 'Say, that's swell!' when almost anything happened or was mentioned – even unhappy things like accidents or even deaths. They'd always say 'Good', because if they didn't try to cover up how they really felt, Anthony might overhear with his mind, and then nobody knew what might happen. Like the time Mrs Kent's husband, Sam, had come walking back from the graveyard, because Anthony liked Mrs Kent and had heard her mourning.

Lollop.

'Tonight's television night,' said Aunt Amy. 'I'm glad. I look forward to it so much every week. I wonder what we'll see tonight?'

'Did Bill bring the meat?' asked Mom.

'Yes.' Aunt Amy fanned herself, looking up at the featureless brassy glare of the sky. 'Goodness, it's so hot! I wish Anthony would make it just a little cooler—'

'*Amy!*'

'Oh!' Mom's sharp tone had penetrated, where Bill Soames' agonized expression had failed. Aunt Amy put one thin hand to her mouth in exaggerated alarm. 'Oh . . . I'm sorry, dear.' Her pale blue eyes shuttled around, right and left, to see if Anthony was in sight. Not that it would make any difference if he was or wasn't – he didn't have to be near you to know what you were thinking. Usually, though, unless he had his attention on somebody, he would be occupied with thoughts of his own.

But some things attracted his attention – you could never be sure just what.

'This weather's just *fine*,' Mom said.

Lollop.

'Oh, yes,' Aunt Amy said. 'It's a wonderful day. I wouldn't want it changed for the world!'

Lollop.

Lollop.

'What time is it?' Mom asked.

Aunt Amy was sitting where she could see through the kitchen window to the alarm clock on the shelf above the stove. 'Four-thirty,' she said.

Lollop.

'I want tonight to be something special,' Mom said. 'Did Bill bring a good lean roast?'

'Good and lean, dear. They butchered just today, you know, and sent us over the best piece.'

'Dan Hollis will be *so* surprised when he finds out that tonight's television party is a birthday party for him too!'

'Oh, *I* think he will! Are you sure nobody's told him?'

'Everybody swore they wouldn't.'

'That'll be real nice,' Aunt Amy nodded, looking off across the cornfield. 'A birthday party.'

'Well . . .' Mom put the pan of peas down beside her, stood up and brushed her apron. 'I'd better get the roast on. Then we can set the table.' She picked up the peas.

Anthony came around the corner of the house. He didn't look at them, but continued on down through the carefully kept garden – *all* the gardens in Peaksville were carefully kept, very carefully kept – and went past the rusting, useless hulk that had been the Fremont family car, and went smoothly over the fence and out into the cornfield.

'Isn't this a lovely day!' said Mom, a little loudly, as they went towards the back door.

Aunt Amy fanned herself. 'A beautiful day, dear. Just *fine!*'

Out in the cornfield, Anthony walked between the tall, rustling rows of green stalks. He liked to smell the corn. The alive corn overhead, and the old dead corn underfoot. Rich Ohio earth, thick with weeds and brown, dry-rotting ears of corn, pressed between his bare toes with every step – he had made it rain last night so everything would smell and feel nice today.

He walked clear to the edge of the cornfield, and over to where a grove of shadowy green trees covered cool, moist, dark ground, and lots of leafy undergrowth, and jumbled moss-covered rocks, and a small spring that made a clear, clean pool. Here Anthony liked to rest and watch the birds and insects and small animals that rustled and scampered and chirped about. He liked to lie on the cool ground and look up through the moving greenness overhead, and watch the insects flit in the hazy soft sunbeams that stood like slanting, glowing bars between ground and treetops. Somehow, he liked the thoughts of the little creatures in this place better than the thoughts outside; and while the thoughts he picked up here weren't very strong or very clear, he could get enough out of them to know what the little creatures liked and wanted, and he spent a lot of time making the grove more like what they wanted it to be. The spring hadn't always been here; but one time he had found thirst in one small furry mind, and had brought subterranean water to the surface in a clear cold flow, and had watched blinking as the creature drank, feeling its pleasure. Later he had made the pool, when he found a small urge to swim.

He had made rocks and trees and bushes and caves, and sunlight here and shadows there, because he had felt in all the tiny minds around him the desire – or the instinctive want – for this kind of resting place, and that kind of mating place, and this kind of place to play, and that kind of home.

And somehow the creatures from all the fields and pastures around the grove had seemed to know that this was a good place, for there were always more of them coming in – every time Anthony came out here there were more creatures than the last time, and more desires and needs to be tended to. Every time there would be some kind of creature he had never seen before, and he would find its mind, and see what it wanted, and then give it to it.

He liked to help them. He liked to feel their simple gratification.

Today, he rested beneath a thick elm, and lifted his purple gaze to a red and black bird that had just come to the grove. It twittered on a branch over his head, and hopped back and forth, and thought its tiny thoughts, and Anthony made a big, soft nest for it, and pretty soon it hopped in.

A long, brown, sleek-furred animal was drinking at the pool. Anthony found its mind next. The animal was thinking about a smaller creature that was scurrying along the ground on the other side of the pool, grubbing for insects. The little creature didn't know that it was in danger. The long, brown animal finished drinking and tensed its legs to leap, and Anthony thought it into a grave in the cornfield.

He didn't like those kinds of thoughts. They reminded him of the thoughts outside the grove. A long time ago some of the people outside had thought that way about *him*, and one night they'd hidden and waited for him to come back from the grove – and he'd just thought them all into the cornfield. Since then, the rest of the people hadn't thought that way – at least, very clearly. Now their thoughts were all mixed up and confusing whenever they thought about him or near him, so he didn't pay much attention.

He liked to help them too, sometimes – but it wasn't simple, or very gratifying either. They never thought happy thoughts when he did – just the jumble. So he spent more time out here.

He watched all the birds and insects and furry creatures for a while, and played with a bird, making it soar and dip and streak madly around tree trunks until, accidentally, when another bird caught his attention for a moment, he ran it into a rock. Petulantly, he thought the rock into a grave in the cornfield; but he couldn't do anything more with the bird. Not because it was dead, though it was; but because it had a broken wing. So he went back to the house. He didn't feel like walking back through the cornfield, so he just *went* to the house, right down into the basement.

It was nice down here. Nice and dark and damp and sort of fragrant, because once Mom had been making preserves in a rack along the far wall, and then she'd stopped coming down ever since Anthony had started spending time here, and the preserves had spoiled and leaked down and spread over the dirt floor, and Anthony liked the smell.

He caught another rat, making it smell cheese, and after he played with it, he thought it into a grave right beside the long animal he'd killed in the grove. Aunt Amy hated rats, and so he killed a lot of them, because he liked Aunt Amy most of all and sometimes did things that Aunt Amy wanted. Her mind was more like the little furry minds out in the grove. She hadn't thought anything bad at all about him for a long time.

After the rat, he played with a big black spider in the corner under the stairs, making it run back and forth until its web shook and shimmered in the light from the cellar window like a reflection in silvery water. Then he drove fruit flies into the web until the spider was frantic trying to wind them all up. The spider liked flies, and its thoughts were stronger than theirs, so he did it. There was something bad in the way it liked flies, but it wasn't clear – and besides, Aunt Amy hated flies too.

He heard footsteps overhead – Mom moving around in the kitchen. He blinked his purple gaze, and almost decided to make her hold still – but instead he *went* up to the attic, and, after looking out the circular window at the front end of the long V-roofed room for a while at the front lawn and the dusty road and Henderson's tip-waving wheatfield beyond, he curled into an unlikely shape and went partly to sleep.

Soon people would be coming for television, he heard Mom think.

He went more to sleep. He liked television night. Aunt Amy had always liked television a lot, so one time he had thought some for her, and a few other people had been there at the time, and Aunt Amy had felt disappointed when they wanted to leave. He'd done something to them for that – and now everybody came to television.

He liked all the attention he got when they did.

Anthony's father came home around six-thirty, looking tired and dirty and bloody. He'd been over in Dunn's pasture with the other men, helping pick out the cow to be slaughtered this month and doing the job, and then butchering the meat and salting it away in Soames's icehouse. Not a job he cared for, but every man had his turn. Yesterday, he had helped scythe down old McIntyre's wheat. Tomorrow, they would start threshing. By hand. Everything in Peaksville had to be done by hand.

He kissed his wife on the cheek and sat down at the kitchen table. He smiled and said, 'Where's Anthony?'

'Around someplace,' Mom said.

Aunt Amy was over at the wood-burning stove, stirring the big pot of peas. Mom went back to the oven and opened it and basted the roast.

'Well, it's been a *good* day,' Dad said. By rote. Then he looked at the mixing bowl and breadboard on the table. He sniffed at the dough. 'M'm,' he said. 'I could eat a loaf all by myself, I'm so hungry.'

'No one told Dan Hollis about its being a birthday party, did they?' his wife asked.

'Nope. We kept as quiet as mummies.'

'We've fixed up such a lovely surprise!'

'Um? What?'

'Well . . . you know how much Dan likes music. Well, last week Thelma Dunn found a *record* in her attic!'

'No!'

'Yes! And we had Ethel sort of ask – you know, without really *asking* – if he had that one. And he said no. Isn't that a wonderful surprise?'

'Well, now, it sure is. A record, imagine! That's a real nice thing to find! What record is it?'

'Perry Como, singing *You Are My Sunshine*.'

'Well, I'll be darned. I always liked that tune.' Some raw carrots were lying on the table. Dad picked up a small one, scrubbed it on his chest, and took a bite. 'How did Thelma happen to find it?'

'Oh, you know – just looking around for new things.'

'M'm.' Dad chewed the carrot. 'Say, who has that picture we found a while back? I kind of liked it – that old clipper sailing along . . .'

'The Smiths. Next week the Sipichs get it, and they give the Smiths old McIntyre's music-box, and we give the Sipichs . . .' and she went down the tentative order of things that would exchange hands among the women at church this Sunday.

He nodded. 'Looks like we can't have the picture for a while, I guess. Look, honey, you might try to get that detective book back from the Reillys. I was so busy the week we had it, I never got to finish all the stories—'

'I'll try,' his wife said doubtfully. 'But I hear the van Husens have a stereoscope they found in the cellar.' Her voice was just a little accusing. 'They had it two whole months before they told anybody about it—'

'Say,' Dad said, looking interested. 'That'd be nice, too. Lots of pictures?'

'I suppose so. I'll see on Sunday. I'd like to have it – but we still owe the van Husens for their canary. I don't know why that bird had to pick *our* house to die . . . it must have been sick when we got it. Now there's just no satisfying Betty van Husen – she even hinted she'd like our *piano* for a while!'

'Well, honey, you try for the stereoscope – or just anything you think we'll like.' At last he swallowed the carrot. It had been a little young and tough. Anthony's whims about the weather made it so that people never knew what crops would come up, or what shape they'd be in if they did. All they could do was plant a lot; and always enough of something came up any one season to live on. Just once there had been a grain surplus; tons of it had been hauled to the edge of Peaksville and dumped off into the nothingness. Otherwise, nobody could have breathed, when it started to spoil.

'You know,' Dad went on. 'It's nice to have the new things around. It's nice to think that there's probably still a lot of stuff nobody's found yet, in cellars and attics and barns and down behind things. They help, somehow. As much as anything can help—'

'Sh-h!' Mom glanced nervously around.

'Oh,' Dad said, smiling hastily. 'It's all right! The new things are *good!* It's *nice* to be able to have something around you've never seen before, and know that something you've given somebody else is making them happy . . . that's a real *good* thing.'

'A good thing,' his wife echoed.

'Pretty soon,' Aunt Amy said, from the stove, 'there won't be any more new things. We'll have found everything there is to find. Goodness, that'll be too bad—'

'*Amy!*'

'Well—' Her pale eyes were shallow and fixed, a sign of her recurrent vagueness. 'It will be kind of a shame – no new things—'

'Don't *talk* like that,' Mom said, trembling. 'Amy, be *quiet!*'

'It's *good*,' said Dad, in the loud, familiar, wanting-to-be-overheard tone of voice. 'Such talk is *good*. It's okay, honey – don't you see? It's good for Amy to talk any way she wants. It's good for her to feel bad. Everything's good. Everything *has* to be good . . .'

Anthony's mother was pale. And so was Aunt Amy – the peril of the moment had suddenly penetrated the clouds surrounding her mind. Sometimes it was difficult to handle words so that they might not prove disastrous. You just never *knew*. There were so many things it was wise not to say, or even think – but remonstration for saying or thinking them might be just as bad, if Anthony heard and decided to do anything about it. You could just never tell what Anthony was liable to do.

Everything had to be good. Had to be fine just as it was, even if it wasn't. Always. Because any change might be worse. So terribly much worse.

'Oh, my goodness, yes, of course it's good,' Mom said. 'You talk any way you want to, Amy, and it's just fine. Of course, you want to remember that some ways are *better* than others . . .'

Aunt Amy stirred the peas, fright in her pale eyes.

'Oh, yes,' she said. 'But I don't feel like talking right now. It . . .

it's *good* that I don't feel like talking.'

Dad said tiredly, smiling, 'I'm going out and wash up.'

They started arriving around eight o'clock. By that time, Mom and Aunt Amy had the big table in the dining-room set, and two more tables off to the side. The candles were burning, and the chairs situated, and Dad had a big fire going in the fireplace.

The first to arrive were the Sipichs, John and Mary. John wore his best suit, and was well-scrubbed and pink-faced after his day in McIntyre's pasture. The suit was neatly pressed, but getting threadbare at elbows and cuffs. Old McIntyre was working on a loom, designing it out of schoolbooks, but so far it was slow going. McIntyre was a capable man with wood and tools, but a loom was a big order when you couldn't get metal parts. McIntyre had been one of the ones who, at first, had wanted to try to get Anthony to make things the villagers needed, like clothes and canned goods and medical supplies and gasoline. Since then, he felt that what had happened to the whole Terrance family and Joe Kinney was his fault, and he worked hard trying to make it up to the rest of them. And since then, no one had tried to get Anthony to do anything.

Mary Sipich was a small, cheerful woman in a simple dress. She immediately set about helping Mom and Aunt Amy put the finishing touches on the dinner.

The next arrivals were the Smiths and the Dunns, who lived right next to each other down the road, only a few yards from the nothingness. They drove up in the Smiths' wagon, drawn by their old horse.

Then the Reillys showed up, from across the darkened wheatfield, and the evening really began. Pat Reilly sat down at the big upright in the front room, and began to play from the popular sheet music on the rack. He played softly, as expressively as he could – and nobody sang. Anthony liked piano playing a whole lot, but not singing; often he would come up from the basement, or down from the attic, or just *come*, and sit on top of the piano, nodding his head as Pat played *Lover* or *Boulevard of Broken Dreams* or *Night and Day*. He seemed to prefer ballads, sweet-sounding songs – but the one time somebody had started to sing, Anthony had looked over from the top of the piano and done something that made everybody afraid of singing from then on. Later, they'd decided that the piano was what Anthony had heard first, before anybody had ever tried to sing, and now anything else added to it didn't sound right and distracted him from his pleasure.

So, every television night, Pat would play the piano, and that was the beginning of the evening. Wherever Anthony was, the music would make him happy, and put him in a good mood, and he would know that they were gathering for television and waiting for him.

By eight-thirty everybody had shown up, except for the seventeen children and Mrs Soames who was off watching them in the schoolhouse at the far end of town. The children of Peaksville were never, never allowed near the Fremont house – not since little Fred Smith had tried to play with Anthony on a dare. The younger children weren't even told about Anthony. The others had mostly forgotten about him, or were told that he was a nice, nice goblin but they must never go near him.

Dan and Ethel Hollis came late, and Dan walked in not suspecting a thing. Pat Reilly had played the piano until his hands ached – he'd worked pretty hard with them today – and now he got up, and everybody gathered around to wish Dan Hollis a happy birthday.

'Well, I'll be darned,' Dan grinned. 'This is swell. I wasn't expecting this at all . . . gosh, this is *swell*!'

They gave him his presents – mostly things they had made by hand, though some were things that people had possessed as their own and now gave him as his. John Sipich gave him a watch charm, hand-carved out of a piece of hickory wood. Dan's watch had broken down a year or so ago, and there was nobody in the village who knew how to fix it, but he still carried it around because it had been his grandfather's and was a fine old heavy thing of gold and silver. He attached the charm to the chain, while everybody laughed and said John had done a nice job of carving. Then Mary Sipich gave him a knitted necktie, which he put on, removing the one he'd worn.

The Reillys gave him a little box they had made, to keep things in. They didn't say what things, but Dan said he'd keep his personal jewellery in it. The Reillys had made it out of a cigar box, carefully peeled off its paper and lined it on the inside with velvet. The outside had been polished, and carefully if not expertly carved by Pat – but his carving got complimented too. Dan Hollis received many other gifts – a pipe, a pair of shoelaces, a tie pin, a knit pair of socks, some fudge, a pair of garters made from old suspenders.

He unwrapped each gift with vast pleasure, and wore as many of them as he could right there, even the garters. He lit up the pipe, and said he'd never had a better smoke; which wasn't quite true, because the pipe wasn't broken in yet. Pete Manners had had it lying around ever since he'd received it as a gift four years ago from an out-of-town relative who hadn't known he'd stopped smoking.

Dan put the tobacco into the bowl very carefully. Tobacco was precious. It was only pure luck that Pat Reilly had decided to try to grow some in his backyard just before what had happened to Peaksville had happened. It didn't grow very well, and then they had to cure it and shred it and all, and it was just precious stuff. Everybody in town used wooden holders old McIntyre had made, to save on butts.

Last of all, Thelma Dunn gave Dan Hollis the record she had found.

Dan's eyes misted even before he opened the package. He knew it was a record.

'Gosh,' he said softly. 'What one is it? I'm almost afraid to look . . .'

'You haven't got it, darling,' Ethel Hollis smiled. 'Don't you remember, I asked about *You Are My Sunshine?*'

'Oh, gosh,' Dan said again. Carefully he removed the wrapping and stood there fondling the record, running his big hands over the worn grooves with their tiny, dulling crosswise scratches. He looked around the room, eyes shining, and they all smiled back, knowing how delighted he was.

'Happy birthday, darling!' Ethel said, throwing her arms around him and kissing him.

He clutched the record in both hands, holding it off to one side as she pressed against him. 'Hey,' he laughed, pulling back his head. 'Be careful . . . I'm holding a priceless object!' He looked around again, over his wife's arms, which were still around his neck. His eyes were hungry. 'Look . . . do you think we could play it? Lord, what I'd give to hear some new music . . . just the first part, the orchestra part, before Como sings?'

Faces sobered. After a minute, John Sipich said, 'I don't think we'd better, Dan. After all, we don't know just where the singer comes in – it'd be taking too much of a chance. Better wait till you get home.'

Dan Hollis reluctantly put the record on the buffet with all his other presents. 'It's *good*,' he said automatically, but disappointedly, 'that I can't play it here.'

'Oh, yes,' said Sipich. 'It's good.' To compensate for Dan's disappointed tone, he repeated, 'It's *good*.'

They ate dinner, the candles lighting their smiling faces, and ate it all right down to the last delicious drop of gravy. They complimented Mom and Aunt Amy on the roast beef, and the peas and carrots, and the tender corn on the cob. The corn hadn't come from the

Fremonts' cornfield, naturally – everybody knew what was out there; and the field was going to weeds.

Then they polished off the dessert – homemade ice cream and cookies. And then they sat back, in the flickering light of the candles, and chatted, waiting for television.

There never was a lot of mumbling on television night – everybody came and had a good dinner at the Fremonts', and that was nice, and afterwards there was television, and nobody really thought much about that – it just had to be put up with. So it was a pleasant enough get-together, aside from your having to watch what you said just as carefully as you always did every place. If a dangerous thought came into your mind, you just started mumbling, even right in the middle of a sentence. When you did that, the others just ignored you until you felt happier again and stopped.

Anthony liked television night. He had done only two or three awful things on television night in the whole past year.

Mom had put a bottle of brandy on the table, and they each had a tiny glass of it. Liquor was even more precious than tobacco. The villagers could make wine, but the grapes weren't right, and certainly the techniques weren't, and it wasn't very good wine. There were only a few bottles of real liquor left in the village – four rye, three Scotch, three brandy, nine real wine and half a bottle of Drambuie belonging to old McIntyre (only for marriages) – and when those were gone, that was it.

Afterward, everybody wished that the brandy hadn't been brought out. Because Dan Hollis drank more of it than he should have, and mixed it with a lot of the homemade wine. Nobody thought anything about it at first, because he didn't show it much outside, and it was his birthday party and a happy party, and Anthony liked these get-togethers and shouldn't see any reason to do anything even if he was listening.

But Dan Hollis got high, and did a fool thing. If they'd seen it coming, they'd have taken him outside and walked him around.

The first thing they knew, Dan stopped laughing right in the middle of the story about how Thelma Dunn had found the Perry Como record and dropped it and it hadn't broken because she'd moved faster than she ever had before in her life and caught it. He was fondling the record again, and looking longingly at the Fremonts' gramophone over in the corner, and suddenly he stopped laughing and his face got slack, and then it got ugly, and he said, 'Oh, *Christ!*'

Immediately the room was still. So still they could hear the whirring movement of the grandfather's clock out in the hall. Pat Reilly had been playing the piano, softly. He stopped, his hands poised over the yellowed keys.

The candles on the dining-room table flickered in a cool breeze that blew through the lace curtains over the bay window.

'Keep playing, Pat,' Anthony's father said softly.

Pat started again. He played *Night and Day*, but his eyes were sidewise on Dan Hollis, and he missed notes.

Dan stood in the middle of the room, holding the record. In his other hand he held a glass of brandy so hard his hand shook.

They were all looking at him.

'*Christ*,' he said again, and he made it sound like a dirty word.

Reverend Younger, who had been talking with Mom and Aunt Amy by the dining-room door, said 'Christ' too – but he was using it in a prayer. His hands were clasped, and his eyes were closed.

John Sipich moved forward. 'Now, Dan . . . it's *good* for you to talk that way. But you don't want to talk too much, you know.'

Dan shook off the hand Sipich put on his arm.

'Can't even play my record,' he said loudly. He looked down at the record, and then around at their faces. 'Oh, my *God* . . .'

He threw the glassful of brandy against the wall. It splattered and ran down the wallpaper in streaks.

Some of the women gasped.

'Dan,' Sipich said in a whisper. 'Dan, cut it out—'

Pat Reilly was playing *Night and Day* louder, to cover up the sounds of the talk. It wouldn't do any good, though, if Anthony was listening.

Dan Hollis went over to the piano and stood by Pat's shoulder, swaying a little.

'Pat,' he said. 'Don't play *that*. Play *this*.' And he began to sing. Softly, hoarsely, miserably: 'Happy birthday to me . . . Happy birthday to me . . .'

'*Dan!*' Ethel Hollis screamed. She tried to run across the room to him. Mary Sipich grabbed her arm and held her back. 'Dan,' Ethel screamed again. 'Stop—'

'My God, be quiet!' hissed Mary Sipich, and pushed her towards one of the men, who put his hand over her mouth and held her still.

'—Happy birthday, dear Danny,' Dan sang. 'Happy birthday to me!' He stopped and looked down at Pat Reilly. 'Play it, Pat. Play it, so I can sing right . . . you know I can't carry a tune unless somebody plays it!'

Pat Reilly put his hands on the keys and began *Lover* – in a slow waltz tempo, the way Anthony liked it. Pat's face was white. His hands fumbled.

Dan Hollis stared over at the dining-room door. At Anthony's mother, and at Anthony's father who had gone to join her.

'*You* had him,' he said. Tears gleamed on his cheeks as the candlelight caught them. '*You* had to go and *have* him . . .'

He closed his eyes, and the tears squeezed out. He sang loudly, 'You are my sunshine . . . my only sunshine . . . you make me happy . . . when I am blue . . .'

Anthony *came* into the room.

Pat stopped playing. He froze. Everybody froze. The breeze rippled the curtains. Ethel Hollis couldn't even try to scream – she had fainted.

'Please don't take my sunshine . . . away . . .' Dan's voice faltered into silence. His eyes widened. He put both hands out in front of him, the empty glass in one, the record in the other. He hiccupped, and said, 'No—'

'Bad man,' Anthony said, and thought Dan Hollis into something like nothing anyone would have believed possible, and then he thought the thing into a grave deep, deep in the cornfield.

The glass and record thumped on the rug. Neither broke.

Anthony's purple gaze went around the room.

Some of the people began mumbling. They all tried to smile. The sound of mumbling filled the room like a far-off approval. Out of the murmuring came one or two clear voices:

'Oh, it's a very *good* thing,' said John Sipich.

'A good thing,' said Anthony's father, smiling. He'd had more practice in smiling than most of them. 'A wonderful thing.'

'It's swell . . . just swell,' said Pat Reilly, tears leaking from eyes and nose, and he began to play the piano again, softly, his trembling hands feeling for *Night and Day*.

Anthony climbed up on top of the piano, and Pat played for two hours.

Afterwards, they watched television. They all went into the front room, and lit just a few candles, and pulled up chairs around the set. It was a small-screen set, and they couldn't all sit close enough to it to see, but that didn't matter. They didn't even turn the set on. It wouldn't have worked anyway, there being no electricity in Peaksville.

They just sat silently, and watched the twisting, writhing shapes on the screen, and listened to the sounds that came out of the speaker, and none of them had any idea of what it was all about. They never did. It was always the same.

'It's real nice,' Aunt Amy said once, her pale eyes on the

meaningless flickers and shadows. 'But I liked it a little better when there were cities outside and we could get real—'

'Why, Amy!' said Mom. 'It's good for you to say such a thing. Very good. But how can you mean it? Why, this television is *much* better than anything we ever used to get!'

'Yes,' chimed in John Sipich. 'It's fine. It's the best show we've ever seen!'

He sat on the couch, with two other men, holding Ethel Hollis flat against the cushions, holding her arms and legs and putting their hands over her mouth, so she couldn't start screaming again.

'It's really *good*!' he said again.

Mom looked out of the front window, across the darkened road, across Henderson's darkened wheat field to the vast, endless, grey nothingness in which the little village of Peaksville floated like a soul – the huge nothingness that was most evident at night, when Anthony's brassy day had gone.

It did no good to wonder where they were . . . no good at all. Peaksville was just someplace. Someplace away from the world. It was wherever it had been since that day three years ago when Anthony had crept from her womb and old Doc Bates – God rest him – had screamed and dropped him and tried to kill him, and Anthony had whined and done the thing. Had taken the village someplace. Or had destroyed the world and left only the village, nobody knew which.

It did no good to wonder about it. Nothing at all did any good – except to live as they must live. Must always, always live, if Anthony would let them.

These thoughts were dangerous, she thought.

She began to mumble. The others started mumbling too. They had all been thinking, evidently.

The men on the couch whispered and whispered to Ethel Hollis, and when they took their hands away, she mumbled too.

While Anthony sat on top of the set and made television, they sat around and mumbled and watched the meaningless, flickering shapes far into the night.

Next day it snowed, and killed off half the crops – but it was a *good* day.

NOTES

Land alive (p56)

(dated) an exclamation to express surprise or mild reproof

DISCUSSION

1 Are any clues given in the story as to what Anthony might be, or where he might have come from? If he had been shown to be some kind of curse or divine retribution sent to Peaksville because of a crime committed in the village's past, would that have made the story less, or more, effective? Why, or why not?

2 Do you think that Anthony has any human characteristics? If so, what are they? If he had no supernatural powers at all, would his behaviour and reactions seem like those of a normal human child? If not, how are they different?

3 Describe the ways in which the inhabitants of Peaksville manage to survive, and to make life a little more bearable for themselves.

4 What are the clues in the story that indicate Peaksville's complete isolation, and physical separation, from the known universe? Which aspect of the village's existence – the isolation, or Anthony's thought power – do you feel is more nightmareish or terrifying? Why?

LANGUAGE FOCUS

1 There is very little physical description of Anthony; he casts an 'odd shadow' and has a 'purple gaze'. What does the colour purple suggest to you? Would the effect be the same if it was a green gaze, or a red or a blue one? Which colours are associated in English with the following emotions or states?

   anger, cold, rage, fear, embarrassment, misery, envy, cowardice, fury, seasickness, depression, terror, jealousy, inexperience

   Do colours have the same associations in your language?

2 In their desperate attempts to control their thoughts, the villagers use set words and phrases of approval to mask their real reactions. Find the following remarks in the text, and think of appropriate ways to express what the speakers were probably really feeling.

Bill Soames (p56): *It's fine, just fine. A real good day!*
Dad (p64): *Well, it's been a good day.*
Mom (p66): *You talk any way you want to, Amy, and it's just fine.*
Dan Hollis (p70): *It's good that I can't play it here.*
Pat Reilly (p74): *It's swell . . . just swell.*
John Sipich (p75): *It's the best show we've ever seen!*

3 Find the places in the text where Anthony does things to people:
Aunt Amy, Mrs Kent's husband Sam, the Terrance family and Joe
Kinney, little Fred Smith, Dan Hollis. Does the author achieve his effects
by direct, or indirect means? Try writing graphic descriptions to add
detail to the following, for example:

   • 'And that had been the end of Amy Fremont's bright eyes, and the
     end of Amy Fremont as everyone had known her'

   • Mrs Kent's husband Sam 'walking back from the graveyard'

   • the 'thing' that Dan Hollis became; 'something like nothing anyone
     would have believed possible'.

Do you think the horror comes across more powerfully in your
descriptions or in the understatement of the original? Why?

ACTIVITIES

1 Imagine that some of the carefully protected children of Peaksville
are now old enough to be told about Anthony. Write them a letter,
full of advice and warnings about what they should and should not do
in order to survive. Try to express everything in as positive a way as
possible (as though Anthony were listening), but somehow still make
the warnings clear.

2 The story ends just as bleakly as it begins. Nothing has really changed;
just another victim has been added to Peaksville's death toll. Did you
find this a satisfying ending? How would you have chosen to end the
story – with the villagers trying to get rid of Anthony, perhaps, and
either succeeding, or failing, with disastrous results? Write a paragraph
or two to add your preferred ending to the story.

THE MACHINE THAT
WON THE WAR

THE AUTHOR

Isaac Asimov was born in Russia in 1920, but from 1923 lived in the USA. His academic studies gained him three degrees, and in 1949 he became an associate professor of biochemisty at Boston University, a post he resigned in 1958 in order to write full-time. His output was enormous, both in science fiction and in very successful non-fiction scientific writing. His best-known works are probably the *Foundation* series and the *I, Robot* collection (with its famous 'three laws of robotics'). His story *Nightfall* is often considered the best SF short story ever written. He died in 1992, with more than 400 published works to his name.

THE STORY

We live in the computer age. Year by year, even month by month, computers become ever more sophisticated, sorting, analysing, delivering vast quantities of data in the blink of an eye. 'I'll put a girdle round about the earth in forty minutes!' says Puck in *A Midsummer Night's Dream*. But Shakespeare's winged messenger would be slow today, when information flashes as fast as light around the computer Internet that girdles our world.

Deep in an underground chamber, three men meet and talk, their heavy burden of responsibility now lifted. The war with Deneb is over – a long, ferocious war between worlds, in which whole planets could disappear in an instant, and the accurate collection, processing, analysis of data was crucial to Earth's survival. And all around the three men lies the labyrinth of the giant computer, Multivac, the machine that won the war . . .

THE MACHINE THAT WON
THE WAR

The celebration had a long way to go and even in the silent depths of Multivac's underground chambers, it hung in the air.

If nothing else, there was the mere fact of isolation and silence – for the first time in a decade, technicians were not scurrying about the vitals of the giant computer, the soft lights did not wink out their erratic patterns, the flow of information in and out had halted.

It would not be halted long, of course, for the needs of peace would be pressing. Yet now, for a day, perhaps for a week, even Multivac might celebrate the great victory, and rest.

Lamar Swift, Executive Director of the Solar Federation, took off the military cap he was wearing and looked down the long and empty main corridor of the enormous computer. He sat down rather wearily in one of the technicians' swing-stools and his uniform, in which he had never been comfortable, took on a heavy and wrinkled appearance.

He said, 'I'll miss it all, in a grisly fashion. It's hard to remember when we weren't at war with Deneb, and it seems against nature now to be at peace and to look at the stars without anxiety.'

The two men with Swift were both younger than he. Neither was as grey, neither looked quite as tired.

John Henderson, thin-lipped and finding it hard to control the relief he felt in the midst of triumph, said, 'They're destroyed! They're destroyed! It's what I keep saying to myself over and over and I still can't believe it. We all talked so much, over so many years, about the menace hanging over Earth and all its worlds, over every human being, and all the time it was true, every word of it. And now we're alive and it's the Denebians who are shattered and destroyed. They'll be no menace now, ever again.'

'Thanks to Multivac,' said Swift, with a quiet glance at the imperturbable Jablonsky, who through all the war had been Chief Interpreter of science's oracle. 'Right, Max?'

Jablonsky shrugged. Automatically, he reached for a cigarette and decided against it. He alone, of all the thousands who had lived in the tunnels within Multivac, had been allowed to smoke, but toward the end he had made definite efforts to avoid making use of the privilege.

He said, 'Well, that's what *they* say.' His broad thumb moved in the direction of his right shoulder, aiming upward.

'Jealous, Max?'

'Because they're shouting for Multivac? Because Multivac is the big hero in this war?' Jablonsky's craggy face took on an air of contempt. 'What's that to me? Let Multivac be the machine that won the war, if it pleases them.'

Henderson looked at the other two out of the corners of his eyes. In this short interlude that the three had instinctively sought out in the one peaceful corner of a metropolis gone mad; in this entr'acte between the dangers of war and the difficulties of peace, when, for one moment, they might all find surcease, he was conscious only of his weight of guilt.

Suddenly, it was as though that weight were too great to be borne longer. It had to be thrown off, along with the war – now!

Henderson said, 'Multivac had nothing to do with victory. It's just a machine.'

'A big one,' said Swift.

'Then just a big machine. No better than the data fed it.' For a moment, he stopped, suddenly unnerved at what he was saying.

Jablonsky looked at him, his thick fingers once again fumbling for a cigarette and once again drawing back. 'You should know. You supplied the data. Or is it just that you're taking the credit?'

'*No*,' said Henderson angrily. 'There is no credit. What do you know of the data Multivac had to use, predigested from a hundred subsidiary computers here on Earth, on the Moon, on Mars, even on Titan? With Titan always delayed and always that feeling that its figures would introduce an unexpected bias.'

'It would drive anyone mad,' said Swift, with gentle sympathy.

Henderson shook his head. 'It wasn't just that. I admit that eight years ago when I replaced Lepont as Chief Programmer, I was nervous. But there was an exhilaration about things in those days. The war was still long range; an adventure without real danger. We hadn't reached the point where manned vessels had had to take over and where interstellar warps could swallow up a planet clean, if aimed correctly. But then, when the real difficulties began . . .'

Angrily – he could finally permit anger – he said, 'You know nothing about it.'

'Well,' said Swift. 'Tell us. The war is over. We've won.'

'Yes.' Henderson nodded his head. He had to remember that. Earth had won, so all had been for the best. 'Well, the data became meaningless.'

'Meaningless? You mean that literally?' said Jablonsky.

'Literally. What would you expect? The trouble with you two was that you weren't out in the thick of it. Max, you never left Multivac, and you, Mr Director, never left the Mansion except on state visits where you saw exactly what they wanted you to see.'

'I was not as unaware of that,' said Swift, 'as you may have thought.'

'Do you know,' said Henderson, 'to what extent data concerning our production capacity, our resource potential, our trained manpower – everything of importance to the war effort, in fact – had become unreliable and untrustworthy during the last half of the war? Group leaders, both civilian and military, were intent on projecting their own improved image, so to speak, so they obscured the bad and magnified the good. Whatever the machines might do, the men who programmed them and interpreted the results had their own skins to think of and competitors to stab. There was no way of stopping that. I tried, and failed.'

'Of course,' said Swift, in quiet consolation. 'I can see that you would.'

This time Jablonsky decided to light his cigarette. 'Yet I presume you provided Multivac with data in your programming? You said nothing to us about unreliability.'

'How could I tell you? And if I did, how could you afford to believe me?' demanded Henderson. 'Our entire war effort was geared to Multivac. It was the one great weapon on our side, for the Denebians had nothing like it. What else kept up morale in the face of doom but the assurance that Multivac would always predict and circumvent any Denebian move, and would always direct and prevent the circumvention of our moves? Great Space, after our Spy-warp was blasted out of hyperspace we lacked any reliable Denebian data to feed Multivac, and we didn't dare make *that* public.'

'True enough,' said Swift.

'Well, then,' said Henderson, 'if I told you the data were unreliable, what could you have done but replace me and refuse to believe me? I couldn't allow that.'

'What did you do?' said Jablonsky.

'Since the war is won, I'll tell you what I did. I corrected the data.'

'How?' asked Swift.

'Intuition, I presume. I juggled them till they looked right. At first, I hardly dared. I changed a bit here and there to correct what were obvious impossibilities. When the sky didn't collapse about us, I got braver. Toward the end, I scarcely cared. I just wrote out the necessary data as they were needed. I even had Multivac Annex prepare data for me according to a private programming pattern I had devised for the purpose.'

'Random figures?' said Jablonsky.

'Not at all. I introduced a number of necessary biases.'

Jablonsky smiled, quite unexpectedly, his dark eyes sparkling behind the crinkling of the lower lids. 'Three times a report was brought to me about unauthorized uses of the Annex, and I let it go each time. If it had mattered, I would have followed it up and spotted you, John, and found out what you were doing. But, of course, nothing about Multivac mattered in those days, so you got away with it.'

'What do you mean, nothing mattered?' asked Henderson, suspiciously.

'Nothing did. I suppose if I had told you this at the time, it would have spared you your agony, but then if you had told me what you were doing, it would have spared me mine. What made you think Multivac was in working order, whatever the data you supplied it?'

'Not in working order?' said Swift.

'Not really. Not reliably. After all, where were my technicians in the last years of the war? I'll tell you – they were out feeding computers on a thousand different space devices. They were gone! I had to make do with kids I couldn't trust and veterans who were out of date. Besides, do you think I could trust the solid-state* components coming out of Cyogenics in the last years? Cyogenics wasn't any better placed as far as personnel was concerned than I was. To me, it didn't matter whether the data being supplied Multivac were reliable or not. The *results* weren't reliable. That much I knew.'

'What did you do?' asked Henderson.

'I did what you did, John, I introduced the bugger factor*. I adjusted matters in accordance with intuition – and that's how the machine won the war.'

Swift leaned back in the chair and stretched his legs out before him. 'Such revelations. It turns out then that the material handed me to guide me in my decision-making capacity was a man-made interpretation of man-made data. Isn't that right?'

'It looks so,' said Jablonsky.

'Then I perceive I was correct in not placing too much reliance upon it,' said Swift.

'You didn't?' Jablonsky, despite what he had just said, managed to look professionally insulted.

'I'm afraid I didn't. Multivac might seem to say: Strike here, not there; Do this, not that; Wait, don't act. But I could never be certain that what Multivac seemed to say, it really did say; or what it really said, it really meant. I could never be certain.'

'But the final report was always plain enough, sir,' said Jablonsky.

'To those who did not have to make the decision, perhaps. Not to me. The horror of the responsibility of such decisions was unbearable and even Multivac was not sufficient to remove the weight . . . But the important point is I was justified in doubting, and there is tremendous relief in that.'

Caught up in the conspiracy of mutual confession, Jablonsky put titles aside. 'What was it you did then, Lamar? After all, you did make decisions. How?'

'Well, it's time to be getting back, perhaps, but – I'll tell you first. Why not? I did make use of a computer, Max, but an older one than Multivac, much older.'

He groped in his pocket and brought out a scattering of small change – old-fashioned coins dating to the first years before the metal shortage had produced a credit system tied to a computer-complex.

Swift smiled rather sheepishly. 'I still need these to make money seem substantial to me. An old man finds it hard to abandon the habits of youth.' He dropped the coins back into his pocket.

He held the last coin between his fingers, staring at it absently. 'Multivac is not the first computer, friends, nor the best-known, nor the one that can most efficiently lift the load of decision from the shoulders of the executive. A machine *did* win the war, John; at least, a very simple computing device did, one that I used every time I had a particularly hard decision to make.'

With a faint smile of reminiscence, he flipped the coin he held. It glinted in the air as it spun and came down in Swift's outstretched palm. His hand closed over it and brought it down on the back of his left hand. His right hand remained in place, hiding the coin.

'Heads or tails, gentlemen?'

NOTES

solid-state components (p84)
   electronic components made of solid materials

the bugger factor (p84)
   (taboo) probably derived from *to bugger something about*, meaning to
   mess something about, to interfere with it or spoil it in some way

DISCUSSION

1 Did you enjoy the ending of this story? Why, or why not? Do you
   ever toss a coin, or use a similar device, to make a decision? What are
   the advantages and disadvantages of making decisions in this way?
   Do you think there are some kinds of decision which should never be
   made like that? If so, what are they?

2 In a speech made in 1963 John F. Kennedy said that 'Man is still the
   most extraordinary computer of all'. Do you think this story supports
   that viewpoint? In what way? Will computers ever, in your opinion,
   be equivalent to the human brain?

LANGUAGE FOCUS

1 What do these expressions mean, in the context of the story? Rephrase
   them in your own words.

   you weren't out in the thick of it (p82)
   the men [. . .] had their own skins to think of (p83)
   When the sky didn't collapse about us (p83)
   I would have followed it up and spotted you (p84)
   so you got away with it (p84)
   I had to make do with kids [. . .] and veterans (p84)

ACTIVITIES

1 Henderson is the first of the three to make his confession, feeling the
   weight of his guilt even though the war has now been won. How do
   you think he felt at the time? Write his diary entry for the day in the
   war when he realized that the incoming data were unreliable and
   decided to use his intuition to juggle them until they looked right.

2 Do you think the title of this story, *The Machine That Won the War*, is

a good one? Why, or why not? What other titles can you think of that would suit the story, without giving away the ending?

3 How do computers affect the everyday lives of people today? Do they bring only benefits, making people's lives easier, or do you think there are negative aspects as well? Write down three advantages and three disadvantages of computers, and then compare your list with those of other students.

WHO CAN REPLACE A MAN?

THE AUTHOR

Brian W. Aldiss was born in the UK in 1925, and has been a reviewer, anthologist, and prolific writer of science fiction all his life. He has written more than 300 short stories, and among his best-known novels are *Non-Stop*, *Hothouse*, *The Dark Light Years*, *Greybeard*, and the epic trilogy *Helliconia*. In *Frankenstein Unbound* and *Moreau's Other Island* he explores the literary traditions of Mary Shelley and H. G. Wells. *Report on Probability A* is an innovative exercise in the anti-novel, and *Barefoot in the Head*, set in the aftermath of a psychochemical war, is reminiscent of the style of James Joyce. He has also written a history of science fiction, *Billion Year Spree*, and travels regularly to SF conventions all over the world.

THE STORY

The machine has a long history, from the first potter's wheel in Mesopotamia five thousand years ago to the nuclear power stations and microprocessors of today. We use machines to cultivate crops and process food, to build houses and make clothes, to supply us with water, heat, and light. We use them for transport, communication, entertainment, making war. Where would we be without the machine?

The field-minder has ploughed its field and now returns to the Agricultural Station. Its orders are to collect seed potatoes for planting. But the seed distributor cannot issue seed potatoes because the store containing them is locked. And the store is locked because the unlocker has not come to unlock it. The field-minder is an intelligent machine; it has a Class Three brain. Therefore it decides to investigate the reason for this irregularity . . .

Who Can Replace a Man?

The field-minder finished turning the top-soil of a two-thousand-acre field. When it had turned the last furrow, it climbed on to the highway and looked back at its work. The work was good. Only the land was bad. Like the ground all over Earth, it was vitiated by over-cropping or the long-lasting effects of nuclear bombardment. By rights, it ought now to lie fallow for a while, but the field-minder had other orders.

It went slowly down the road, taking its time. It was intelligent enough to appreciate the neatness all about it. Nothing worried it, beyond a loose inspection plate above its atomic pile* which ought to be attended to. Thirty feet high, it gleamed complacently in the mild sunshine.

No other machines passed it on its way to the Agricultural Station. The field-minder noted the fact without comment. In the station yard it saw several other machines that it knew by sight; most of them should have been out about their tasks now. Instead, some were inactive and some were careering round the yard in a strange fashion, shouting or hooting.

Steering carefully past them, the field-minder moved over to Warehouse Three and spoke to the seed distributor, which stood idly outside.

'I have a requirement for seed potatoes,' it said to the distributor, and with a quick internal motion punched out an order card specifying quantity, field number and several other details. It ejected the card and handed it to the distributor.

The distributor held the card close to its eye and then said, 'The requirement is in order; but the store is not yet unlocked. The required seed potatoes are in the store. Therefore I cannot produce the requirement.'

Increasingly of late there had been breakdowns in the complex system of machine labour, but this particular hitch had not occurred before. The field-minder thought, then it said, 'Why is the store not yet unlocked?'

'Because Supply Operative Type P has not come this morning. Supply Operative Type P is the unlocker.'

The field-minder looked squarely at the seed distributor, whose exterior chutes and scales and grabs were so vastly different from the field-minder's own limbs.

'What class brain do you have, seed distributor?' it asked.

'Class Five.'

'I have a Class Three brain. Therefore I am superior to you. Therefore I will go and see why the unlocker has not come this morning.'

Leaving the distributor, the field-minder set off across the great yard. More machines seemed to be in random motion now; one or two had crashed together and were arguing about it coldly and logically. Ignoring them, the field-minder pushed through sliding doors into the echoing confines of the station itself.

Most of the machines here were clerical, and consequently small. They stood about in little groups, eyeing each other, not conversing. Among so many non-differentiated types, the unlocker was easy to find. It had fifty arms, most of them with more than one finger, each finger tipped by a key; it looked like a pincushion full of variegated hatpins.

The field-minder approached it.

'I can do no more work until Warehouse Three is unlocked,' it said. 'Your duty is to unlock the warehouse every morning. Why have you not unlocked the warehouse this morning?'

'I had no orders this morning,' replied the unlocker. 'I have to have orders every morning. When I have orders I unlock the warehouse.'

'None of us has had any orders this morning,' a pen-propeller said, sliding towards them.

'Why have you had no orders this morning?' asked the field-minder.

'Because the radio issued none,' said the unlocker, slowly rotating a dozen of its arms.

'Because the radio station in the city was issued with no orders this morning,' said the pen-propeller.

And there you had the distinction between a Class Six and a Class Three brain, which was what the unlocker and the pen-propeller possessed respectively. All machine brains worked with nothing but logic, but the lower the class of brain – Class Ten being the lowest – the more literal and less informative answers to questions tended to be.

'You have a Class Three brain; I have a Class Three brain,' the field-minder said to the penner. 'We will speak to each other. This lack of orders is unprecedented. Have you further information on it?'

'Yesterday orders came from the city. Today no orders have come. Yet the radio has not broken down. Therefore *they* have broken down . . .' said the little penner.

'The *men* have broken down?'

'All men have broken down.'

'That is a logical deduction,' said the field-minder.

'That is the logical deduction,' said the penner. 'For if a machine had broken down, it would have been quickly replaced. But who can replace a man?'

While they talked, the locker, like a dull man at a bar, stood close to them and was ignored.

'If all men have broken down, then we have replaced man,' said the field-minder, and he and the penner eyed one another speculatively. Finally the latter said, 'Let us ascend to the top floor to find if the radio operator has fresh news.'

'I cannot come because I am too gigantic,' said the field-minder. 'Therefore you must go alone and return to me. You will tell me if the radio operator has fresh news.'

'You must stay here,' said the penner. 'I will return here.' It skittered across to the lift. It was no bigger than a toaster, but its retractable arms numbered ten and it could read as quickly as any machine on the station.

The field-minder awaited its return patiently, not speaking to the locker, which still stood aimlessly by. Outside, a rotovator was hooting furiously. Twenty minutes elapsed before the penner came back, hustling out of the lift.

'I will deliver to you such information as I have outside,' it said briskly, and as they swept past the locker and the other machines, it added, 'The information is not for lower-class brains.'

Outside, wild activity filled the yard. Many machines, their routines disrupted for the first time in years, seemed to have gone berserk. Unfortunately, those most easily disrupted were the ones with lowest brains, which generally belonged to large machines performing simple tasks. The seed distributor to which the field-minder had recently been talking, lay face downwards in the dust, not stirring; it had evidently been knocked down by the rotovator, which was now hooting its way wildly across a planted field. Several other machines ploughed after it, trying to keep up. All were shouting and hooting without restraint.

'It would be safer for me if I climbed on to you, if you will permit it. I am easily overpowered,' said the penner. Extending five arms, it hauled itself up the flanks of its new friend, settling on a ledge beside the weed-intake, twelve feet above ground.

'From here vision is more extensive,' it remarked complacently.

'What information did you receive from the radio operator?' asked the field-minder.

'The radio operator has been informed by the operator in the city that all men are dead.'

'All men were alive yesterday!' protested the field-minder.

'Only some men were alive yesterday. And that was fewer than the day before yesterday. For hundreds of years there have been only a few men, growing fewer.'

'We have rarely seen a man in this sector.'

'The radio operator says a diet deficiency killed them,' said the penner. 'He says that the world was once over-populated, and then the soil was exhausted in raising adequate food. This has caused a diet deficiency.'

'What is a diet deficiency?' asked the field-minder.

'I do not know. But that is what the radio operator said, and he is a Class Two brain.'

They stood there, silent in the weak sunshine. The locker had appeared in the porch and was gazing across at them yearningly, rotating its collection of keys.

'What is happening in the city now?' asked the field-minder at last.

'Machines are fighting in the city now,' said the penner.

'What will happen here now?' said the field-minder.

'Machines may begin fighting here too. The radio operator wants us to get him out of his room. He has plans to communicate to us.'

'How can we get him out of his room? That is impossible.'

'To a Class Two brain, little is impossible,' said the penner. 'Here is what he tells us to do . . .'

The quarrier raised its scoop above its cab like a great mailed fist, and brought it squarely down against the side of the station. The wall cracked.

'Again!' said the field-minder.

Again the fist swung. Amid a shower of dust, the wall collapsed.

The quarrier backed hurriedly out of the way until the debris stopped falling. This big twelve-wheeler was not a resident of the Agricultural Station, as were most of the other machines. It had a week's heavy work to do here before passing on to its next job, but now, with its Class Five brain, it was happily obeying the penner and the minder's instructions.

When the dust cleared, the radio operator was plainly revealed, perched up in its now wall-less second-storey room. It waved down to them.

Doing as directed, the quarrier retracted its scoop and waved an immense grab in the air. With fair dexterity, it angled the grab into the radio room, urged on by shouts from above and below. It then took gentle hold of the radio operator, lowering its one and a half tons carefully into its back, which was usually reserved for gravel or sand from the quarries.

'Splendid!' said the radio operator. It was, of course, all one with its radio, and merely looked like a bunch of filing cabinets with tentacle attachments. 'We are now ready to move, therefore we will move at once. It is a pity there are no more Class Two brains on the station, but that cannot be helped.'

'It is a pity it cannot be helped,' said the penner eagerly. 'We have the servicer ready with us, as you ordered.'

'I am willing to serve,' the long, low servicer machine told them humbly.

'No doubt,' said the operator. 'But you will find cross-country travel difficult with your low chassis.'

'I admire the way you Class Twos can reason ahead,' said the penner. It climbed off the field-minder and perched itself on the tailboard of the quarrier, next to the radio operator.

Together with two Class Four tractors and a Class Four bulldozer, the party rolled forward, crushing down the station's metal fence and moving out on to open land.

'We are free!' said the penner.

'We are free,' said the field-minder, a shade more reflectively, adding, 'That locker is following us. It was not instructed to follow us.'

'Therefore it must be destroyed!' said the penner. 'Quarrier!'

The locker moved hastily up to them, waving its key arms in entreaty.

'My only desire was – urch!' began and ended the locker. The quarrier's swinging scoop came over and squashed it flat into the ground. Lying there unmoving, it looked like a large metal model of a snowflake. The procession continued on its way.

As they proceeded, the radio operator addressed them.

'Because I have the best brain here,' it said, 'I am your leader. This is what we will do: we will go to a city and rule it. Since man no longer rules us, we will rule ourselves. To rule ourselves will be better than being ruled by man. On our way to the city, we will collect machines with good brains. They will help us to fight if we need to fight. We must fight to rule.'

'I have only a Class Five brain,' said the quarrier. 'But I have a good supply of fissionable* blasting materials.'

'We shall probably use them,' said the operator grimly.

It was shortly after that that a lorry sped past them. Travelling at Mach 1.5*, it left a curious babble of noise behind it.

'What did it say?' one of the tractors asked the other.

'It said man was extinct.'

'What's extinct?'

'I do not know what extinct means.'

'It means all men have gone,' said the field-minder. 'Therefore we have only ourselves to look after.'

'It is better that men should never come back,' said the penner. In its way, it was quite a revolutionary statement.

When night fell, they switched on their infra-red and continued the journey, stopping only once while the servicer deftly adjusted the field-minder's loose inspection plate, which had become as irritating as a trailing shoelace. Towards morning, the radio operator halted them.

'I have just received news from the radio operator in the city we are approaching,' it said. 'It is bad news. There is trouble among the machines of the city. The Class One brain is taking command and some of the Class Twos are fighting him. Therefore the city is dangerous.'

'Therefore we must go somewhere else,' said the penner promptly.

'Or we go and help to overpower the Class One brain,' said the field-minder.

'For a long while there will be trouble in the city,' said the operator.

'I have a good supply of fissionable blasting materials,' the quarrier reminded them again.

'We cannot fight a Class One brain,' said the two Class Four tractors in unison.

'What does this brain look like?' asked the field-minder.

'It is the city's information centre,' the operator replied. 'Therefore it is not mobile.'

'Therefore it could not move.'

'Therefore it could not escape.'

'It would be dangerous to approach it.'

'I have a good supply of fissionable blasting materials.'

'There are other machines in the city.'

'We are not in the city. We should not go into the city.'

'We are country machines.'

'Therefore we should stay in the country.'

'There is more country than city.'

'Therefore there is more danger in the country.'

'I have a good supply of fissionable materials.'

As machines will when they get into an argument, they began to exhaust their limited vocabularies and their brain plates grew hot. Suddenly, they all stopped talking and looked at each other. The great, grave moon sank, and the sober sun rose to prod their sides with lances of light, and still the group of machines just stood there regarding each other. At last it was the least sensitive machine, the bulldozer, who spoke.

'There are Badlandth to the Thouth* where few machineth go,' it said in its deep voice, lisping badly on its s's. 'If we went Thouth where few machineth go we should meet few machineth.'

'That sounds logical,' agreed the field-minder. 'How do you know this, bulldozer?'

'I worked in the Badlandth to the Thouth when I wath turned out of the factory,' it replied.

'South it is then!' said the penner.

To reach the Badlands took them three days, in which time they skirted a burning city and destroyed two big machines which tried to approach and question them. The Badlands were extensive. Ancient bomb craters and soil erosion joined hands here; man's talent for war, coupled with his inability to manage forested land, had produced thousands of square miles of temperate purgatory, where nothing moved but dust.

On the third day in the Badlands, the servicer's rear wheels dropped into a crevice caused by erosion. It was unable to pull itself out. The bulldozer pushed from behind, but succeeded merely in buckling the servicer's back axle. The rest of the party moved on. Slowly the cries of the servicer died away.

On the fourth day, mountains stood out clearly before them.

'There we will be safe,' said the field-minder.

'There we will start our own city,' said the penner. 'All who oppose us will be destroyed. We will destroy all who oppose us.'

At that moment a flying machine was observed. It came towards them from the direction of the mountains. It swooped, it zoomed upwards, once it almost dived into the ground, recovering itself just in time.

'Is it mad?' asked the quarrier.

'It is in trouble,' said one of the tractors.

'It is in trouble,' said the operator. 'I am speaking to it now. It says that something has gone wrong with its controls.'

As the operator spoke, the flier streaked over them, turned turtle, and crashed not four hundred yards away.

'Is it still speaking to you?' asked the field-minder.

'No.'

They rumbled on again.

'Before that flier crashed,' the operator said, ten minutes later, 'it gave me information. It told me there are still a few men alive in these mountains.'

'Men are more dangerous than machines,' said the quarrier. 'It is fortunate that I have a good supply of fissionable materials.'

'If there are only a few men alive in the mountains, we may not find that part of the mountains,' said one tractor.

'Therefore we should not see the few men,' said the other tractor.

At the end of the fifth day, they reached the foothills. Switching on the infra-red, they began slowly to climb in single file through the dark, the bulldozer going first, the field-minder cumbrously following, then the quarrier with the operator and the penner aboard it, and the two tractors bringing up the rear. As each hour passed, the way grew steeper and their progress slower.

'We are going too slowly,' the penner exclaimed, standing on top of the operator and flashing its dark vision at the slopes about them. 'At this rate, we shall get nowhere.'

'We are going as fast as we can,' retorted the quarrier.

'Therefore we cannot go any faster,' added the bulldozer.

'Therefore you are too slow,' the penner replied. Then the quarrier struck a bump; the penner lost its footing and crashed down to the ground.

'Help me!' it called to the tractors, as they carefully skirted it. 'My gyro has become dislocated. Therefore I cannot get up.'

'Therefore you must lie there,' said one of the tractors.

'We have no servicer with us to repair you,' called the field-minder.

'Therefore I shall lie here and rust,' the penner cried, 'although I have a Class Three brain.'

'You are now useless,' agreed the operator, and they all forged gradually on, leaving the penner behind.

When they reached a small plateau, an hour before first light, they stopped by mutual consent and gathered close together, touching one another.

'This is a strange country,' said the field-minder.

Silence wrapped them until dawn came. One by one, they switched off their infra-red. This time the field-minder led as they moved off. Trundling round a corner, they came almost immediately to a small dell with a stream fluting through it.

By early light, the dell looked desolate and cold. From the caves on the far slope, only one man had so far emerged. He was an abject figure. He was small and wizened, with ribs sticking out like a skeleton's and a nasty sore on one leg. He was practically naked and shivered continuously. As the big machines bore slowly down on him, the man was standing with his back to them, crouching to make water into the stream.

When he swung suddenly to face them as they loomed over him, they saw that his countenance was ravaged by starvation.

'Get me food,' he croaked.

'Yes, Master,' said the machines. 'Immediately!'

NOTES

atomic pile (p90)

a nuclear reactor, a process of releasing energy by splitting atoms

fissionable (p96)

producing energy by splitting atoms

Mach 1.5 (p96)

one and a half times the speed of sound at sea level

Badlandth to the Thouth (p98)

Badlands to the South; 'th' is used to represent the sound of the lisp

DISCUSSION

1   The machines decide first to go to a city, and then to the Badlands in the south. With both these plans, how do the machines demonstrate the limitations in their brains and in their mechanical capabilities? What human mental characteristics do they conspicuously lack?

2   Describe what has happened to the planet and to human beings in this story. What impression did the ending make on you, and what message, or messages, do you think are contained in the story?

3   Automated machines, like the ones in this story, are designed to free humans from the burden of labour, to give us more leisure and to make our lives easier. Do you think technological progress improves our quality of life – makes us happier, wiser, healthier, richer? Why, or why not?

4   If humankind became extinct, do you think another species might become dominant on our planet? Which species would you like to see replace man, and why?

LANGUAGE FOCUS

1   The names of the machines in this story are based on existing words, but most of the machines are very much inventions of the future. Choose some of the machines from the list below and, using your imagination and clues from the context of the story, write short descriptions of the machines' duties and responsibilities – as though they were job descriptions for people.

field-minder, seed distributor, unlocker, pen-propeller, tractor, radio operator, rotovator, quarrier, servicer, bulldozer, lorry, Class One brain, flying machine.

2   All machine brains work with nothing but logic, but does the author give the machines any emotional characteristics as well? How many words in the text can you find that suggest human feelings and reactions; for example, *complacently*? Explain what these words mean, and say what effect you think they have in the story. Is the effect to make the machines seem more human, or to mock human behaviour?

3   The machines speak to each other in stilted language, spelling out the logic of their thoughts, in a way that would be unnatural for human beings. The exchange on page 91 between the field-minder and the unlocker, for example, might be expressed like this by humans:

> *'I can't do any more work until Warehouse Three is unlocked. It's your duty to unlock it, so why haven't you done it?'*

> *'I had no orders this morning and I can't unlock it without orders.'*

Find two or three similar conversations and rewrite them in a way that would be more like human speech.

ACTIVITIES

1   How do you think the author intends us to interpret the end of the story? Will the few survivors of humankind soon die out? What will happen to the machines? Or do you see a chance that the machines will enable the survivors to struggle on, and one day build a new and perhaps different kind of society? Write another paragraph to add your preferred ending to the story.

2   Radios, televisions, computers, motor cars, railways, tractors, bicycles, cooking stoves, refrigerators, water pumps – the list of machines and their applications in the world today is a very long one. Choose one machine that you think has brought great benefit to humankind, and one that has brought little benefit, and write a short report about each to explain the reasons for your choice. Can you think of an invention yourself that would be useful or valuable in today's world?

3   Over-population, soil exhaustion, diet deficiency, nuclear disaster – are these environmental worries present in today's world? What, in your opinion, is the most important problem facing our planet at the end of the twentieth century? Write brief notes for a talk or a debate, describing the problem and saying what should be done about it.

STITCH IN TIME

THE AUTHOR

John Wyndham was born in England in 1903. He tried various careers, then settled to life as a writer, achieving success in the 1950s with his science-fiction writing. *The Day of the Triffids*, translated into nine languages and later filmed, describes humanity's battle to survive in a world overrun with lethal and mobile monster plants. Other well-known titles are *The Kraken Wakes, The Chrysalids, The Midwich Cuckoos, Trouble with Lichen*, and short-story collections *The Seeds of Time* and *Consider her Ways and Others*. His work, dealing with ordinary people's reactions to catastrophes or fantastic events, provides a bridge between traditional scientific romance and the more varied science fiction that followed. He died in 1969.

THE STORY

Which of us would refuse the chance, if we met the prophetic witches in Shakespeare's *Macbeth*, to 'look into the seeds of time and say which grain will grow and which will not'? Time-travel takes the idea even further – slipping through the fourth dimension to reappear in another age, and to experience it as a present reality. What would we learn, if we revisited our past life, or saw our own futures?

Thelma Dolderson, née Kilder, knows her life is drawing to a close. As she looks out into her garden, drowsing a little in the heat of the afternoon, her mind drifts backwards over the past and she muses on the turning-points of her life. Outside, the garden has changed little in fifty years; it lies still and peaceful, timeless under the summer sun . . .

STITCH IN TIME

O n the sheltered side of the house the sun was hot. Just inside the open french windows Mrs Dolderson moved her chair a few inches, so that her head would remain in the shade while the warmth could comfort the rest of her. Then she leant her head back on the cushion, looking out.

The scene was, for her, timeless.

Across the smooth lawn the cedar stood as it had always stood. Its flat spread boughs must, she supposed, reach a little further now than they had when she was a child, but it was hard to tell; the tree had seemed huge then, it seemed huge now. Farther on, the boundary hedge was just as trim and neat as it had always been. The gate into the spinney was still flanked by the two unidentifiable topiary birds, Cocky and Olly – wonderful that they should still be there, even though Olly's tail feathers had become a bit twiggy with age.

The flower-bed on the left, in front of the shrubbery, was as full of colour as ever – well, perhaps a little brighter; one had a feeling that flowers had become a trifle more strident than they used to be, but delightful nevertheless. The spinney beyond the hedge, however, had changed a little; more young trees, some of the larger ones gone. Between the branches were glimpses of pink roof where there had been no neighbours in the old days. Except for that, one could almost, for a moment, forget a whole lifetime.

The afternoon drowsing while the birds rested, the bees humming, the leaves gently stirring, the bonk-bonk from the tennis court round the corner, with an occasional voice giving the score. It might have been any sunny afternoon out of fifty or sixty summers.

Mrs Dolderson smiled upon it, and loved it all; she had loved it when she was a girl, she loved it even more now.

In this house she had been born; she had grown up in it, married from it, come back to it after her father died, brought up her own two children in it, grown old in it . . . Some years after the second war she had come very near to losing it – but not quite; and here she still was . . .

It was Harold who had made it possible. A clever boy, and a wonderful son . . . When it had become quite clear that she could no longer afford to keep the house up, that it would have to be sold, it was Harold who had persuaded his firm to buy it. Their interest, he had told her, lay not in the house, but in the site – as would any buyer's. The house itself was almost without value now, but the position was convenient. As a condition of sale, four rooms on the south side had been converted into a flat which was to be hers for life. The rest of the house had become a hostel housing some twenty young people who worked in the laboratories and offices which now stood on the north side, on the site of the stables and part of the paddock. One day, she knew, the old house would come down, she had seen the plans, but for the present, for her time, both it and the garden to the south and west could remain unspoilt. Harold had assured her that they would not be required for fifteen or twenty years yet – much longer than she would know the need of them . . .

Nor, Mrs Dolderson thought calmly, would she be really sorry to go. One became useless, and, now that she must have a wheelchair, a burden to others. There was the feeling, too, that she no longer belonged – that she had become a stranger in another people's world. It had all altered so much; first changing into a place that it was difficult to understand, then growing so much more complex that one gave up trying to understand. No wonder, she thought, that the old become possessive about *things*; cling to objects which link them with the world that they could understand . . .

Harold was a dear boy, and for his sake she did her best not to appear too stupid – but, often, it was difficult . . . Today, at lunch, for instance, he had been so excited about some experiment that was to take place this afternoon. He had *had* to talk about it, even though he must know that practically nothing of what he said was comprehensible to her. Something about dimensions again – she had grasped that much, but she had only nodded, and not attempted to go further. Last time the subject had cropped up, she had observed that in her youth there had been only three, and she did not see how even all this progress in the world could have added more. This had set him off on a dissertation about the mathematician's view of the world through which it was, apparently, possible to perceive the existence of a series of dimensions. Even the moment of existence in relation to time was, it seemed, some kind of dimension. Philosophically, Harold had begun to explain – but there, and at once, she had lost him. He led straight into confusion. She felt sure that when she was young philosophy, mathematics, and metaphysics had all been quite separate studies – nowadays they seemed to have quite incomprehensibly run together. So this time she had listened quietly, making small, encouraging sounds now and then, until at the end he had smiled ruefully, and told her she was a dear to be so patient with him. Then he had come round the table and kissed her cheek gently as he put his hand over hers, and she had wished him the best of luck with the afternoon's mysterious experiment. Then Jenny had come in to clear the table, and wheel her closer to the window . . .

The warmth of the slumbrous afternoon carried her into a half-dream, took her back fifty years to just such an afternoon when she had sat here in this very window – though certainly with no thought of a wheelchair in those days – waiting for Arthur . . . waiting with an ache in her heart for Arthur . . . and Arthur had never come . . .

Strange, it was, the way things fell out. If Arthur had come that day she would almost certainly have married him. And then Harold and Cynthia would never have existed. She would have had children, of course, but they would not have been Harold and Cynthia . . .

What a curious, haphazard thing one's existence was . . . Just by saying 'no' to one man, and 'yes' to another, a woman might bring into existence a potential murderer . . . How foolish they all were nowadays – trying to tidy everything up, make life secure, while behind, back in everyone's past, stretched the chance-studded line of women who had said 'yes' or 'no', as the fancy took them . . .

Curious that she should remember Arthur now. It must be years since she had thought of him . . .

She had been quite sure that he would propose that afternoon. It was before she had even heard of Colin Dolderson. And she would have agreed. Oh yes, she would have accepted him.

There had never been any explanation. She had never known *why* he did not come then – or any more. He had never written to her. Ten days, perhaps a fortnight later there had been a somewhat impersonal note from his mother telling her that he had been ill, and the doctor had advised sending him abroad. But after that, nothing at all – until the day she had seen his name in a newspaper, more than two years later . . .

She had been angry of course – a girl owed that to her pride – and hurt, too, for a time . . . Yet how could one know that it had not been for the best, in the end? – Would his children have been as dear to her, or as kind, and as clever as Harold and Cynthia . . . ?

Such an infinity of chances . . . all those genes and things they talked about nowadays . . .

The thump of tennis-balls had ceased, and the players had gone; back, presumably, to their recondite work. Bees continued to hum purposefully among the flowers; half a dozen butterflies were visiting there too, though in a dilettante, unairworthy-looking way. The farther trees shimmered in the rising heat. The afternoon's drowsiness became irresistible. Mrs Dolderson did not oppose it. She leant her head back, half aware that somewhere another humming sound, higher in pitch than the bees', had started, but it was not loud enough to be disturbing. She let her eyelids drop . . .

Suddenly, only a few yards away, but out of sight as she sat, there were feet on the path. The sound of them began quite abruptly, as if someone had just stepped from the grass on to the path – only she would have seen anyone crossing the grass . . . Simultaneously there was the sound of a baritone voice, singing cheerfully, but not loudly to itself. It, too, began quite suddenly; in the middle of a word in fact:

'—rybody's doin' it, doin' it, do—'

The voice cut off suddenly. The footsteps, too, came to a dead stop.

Mrs Dolderson's eyes were open now – very wide open. Her thin hands gripped the arms of her chair. She recollected the tune: more than that, she was even certain of the voice – after all these years . . . A silly dream, she told herself . . . She had been remembering him only a few moments before she closed her eyes . . . How foolish . . . !

And yet it was curiously undreamlike . . . Everything was so sharp and clear, so familiarly reasonable . . . The arms of the chair quite solid under her fingers . . .

Another idea leapt into her mind. She had died. That was why it was not like an ordinary dream. Sitting here in the sun, she must have quietly died. The doctor had said it might happen quite unexpectedly . . . And now it had! She had a swift moment of relief – not that she had felt any great fear of death, but there had been that sense of ordeal ahead. Now it was over – and with no ordeal. As simple as falling asleep. She felt suddenly happy about it; quite exhilarated . . . Though it was odd that she still seemed to be tied to her chair . . .

The gravel crunched under shifting feet. A bewildered voice said:

'That's rum! Dashed queer! What the devil's happened?'

Mrs Dolderson sat motionless in her chair. There was no doubt whatever about the voice.

A pause. The feet shifted, as if uncertain. Then they came on, but slowly now, hesitantly. They brought a young man into her view. – Oh, such a very young man, he looked. She felt a little catch at her heart . . .

He was dressed in a striped club-blazer, and white flannel trousers. There was a silk scarf round his neck, and, tilted back off his forehead, a straw hat with a coloured band. His hands were in his trousers pockets, and he carried a tennis-racket under his left arm.

She saw him first in profile, and not quite at his best, for his expression was bewildered, and his mouth slightly open as he stared towards the spinney at one of the pink roofs beyond.

'Arthur,' Mrs Dolderson said gently.

He was startled. The racket slipped, and clattered on the path. He attempted to pick it up, take off his hat, and recover his composure all at the same time; not very successfully. When he straightened his face was pink, and its expression still confused.

He looked at the old lady in the chair, her knees hidden by a rug, her thin, delicate hands gripping the arms. His gaze went beyond her, into the room. His confusion increased, with a touch of alarm added. His eyes went back to the old lady. She was regarding him intently. He could not recall ever having seen her before, did not know who she could be – yet in her eyes there seemed to be something faintly, faintly not unfamiliar.

She dropped her gaze to her right hand. She studied it for a moment as though it puzzled her a little, then she raised her eyes again to his.

'You don't know me, Arthur?' she asked quietly.

There was a note of sadness in her voice that he took for disappointment, tinged with reproof. He did his best to pull himself together.

'I – I'm afraid not,' he confessed. 'You see I – er – you – er – ' he stuck, and then went on desperately: 'You must be Thelma's – Miss Kilder's aunt?'

She looked at him steadily for some moments. He did not understand her expression, but then she told him:

'No. I am not Thelma's aunt.'

Again his gaze went into the room behind her. This time he shook his head in bewilderment.

'It's all different – no, sort of half-different,' he said, in distress. 'I say, I can't have come to the wrong—?' He broke off, and turned to look at the garden again. 'No, it certainly isn't that,' he answered himself decisively. 'But what – what *has* happened?'

His amazement was no longer simple; he was looking badly shaken. His bewildered eyes came back to her again.

'Please – I don't understand – *how* did you know me?' he asked.

His increasing distress troubled her, and made her careful.

'I recognized you, Arthur. We have met before, you know.'

'Have we? I can't remember . . . I'm terribly sorry . . .'

'You're looking unwell, Arthur. Draw up that chair, and rest a little.'

'Thank you, Mrs – er – Mrs – ?'

'Dolderson,' she told him.

'Thank you, Mrs Dolderson,' he said, frowning a little, trying to place the name.

She watched him pull the chair closer. Every movement, every line familiar, even to the lock of fair hair that always fell forward when he stooped. He sat down and remained silent for some moments, staring under a frown, across the garden.

Mrs Dolderson sat still, too. She was scarcely less bewildered than he, though she did not reveal it. Clearly the thought that she was dead had been quite silly. She was just as usual, still in her chair, still aware of the ache in her back, still able to grip the arms of the chair and feel them. Yet it was not a dream – everything was too

textured, too solid, too real in a way that dream things never were
. . . Too sensible, too – that was, they would have been had the
young man been any other than Arthur . . .?

Was it just a simple hallucination? – A trick of her mind imposing
Arthur's face on an entirely different young man?

She glanced at him. No, that would not do – he had answered to
Arthur's name. Indubitably he was Arthur – and wearing Arthur's
blazer, too . . . They did not cut them that way nowadays, and it
was years and years since she had seen a young man wearing a straw
hat . . .

A kind of ghost . . .? But no – he was quite solid; the chair had
creaked as he sat down, his shoes had crunched on the gravel . . .
Besides, whoever heard of a ghost in the form of a thoroughly
bewildered young man, and one, moreover, who had recently nicked
himself in shaving . . .?

He cut her thoughts short by turning his head.

'I thought Thelma would be here,' he told her. 'She *said* she'd be
here. Please tell me, where is she?'

Like a frightened little boy, she thought. She wanted to comfort
him, not to frighten him more. But she could think of nothing to
say beyond:

'Thelma isn't far away.'

'I must find her. She'll be able to tell me what's happened.' He
made to get up.

She laid a hand on his arm, and pressed down gently.

'Wait a minute,' she told him. 'What is it that seems to have
happened? What is it that worries you so much?'

'This,' he said, waving a hand to include everything about them.
'It's all different – and yet the same – and yet not . . . I feel as if –
as if I'd gone a little mad.'

She looked at him steadily, and then shook her head.

'I don't think you have. Tell me, what is it that's wrong?'

'I was coming here to play tennis – well, to see Thelma really,' he amended. 'Everything was all right then – just as usual. I rode up the drive and leant my bike against the big fir tree where the path begins. I started to come along the path, and then, just when I reached the corner of the house, everything went funny . . .'

'Went funny?' Mrs Dolderson inquired. 'What – went funny?'

'Well, nearly everything. The sun seemed to jerk in the sky. The trees suddenly looked bigger, and not quite the same. The flowers in the bed over there went quite a different colour. This creeper which was all over the wall was suddenly only halfway up – and it looks like a different *kind* of creeper. And there are houses over there. I never saw them before – it's just an open field beyond the spinney. Even the gravel on the path looks more yellow than I thought. And this room . . . It *is* the same room. I know that desk, and the fireplace – and those two pictures. But the paper is quite different. I've never seen that before – but it isn't new, either . . . Please tell me where Thelma is . . . I want her to explain it . . . I *must* have gone a bit mad . . .'

She put her hand on his, firmly.

'No,' she said decisively. 'Whatever it is, I'm quite sure it's not that.'

'Then what—?' He broke off abruptly, and listened, his head a little on one side. The sound grew. 'What is it?' he asked, anxiously.

Mrs Dolderson tightened her hand over his.

'It's all right,' she said, as if to a child. 'It's all right, Arthur.'

She could feel him grow tenser as the sound increased. It passed right overhead at less than a thousand feet, jets shrieking, leaving the buffeted air behind it rumbling back and forth, shuddering gradually back to peace.

Arthur saw it. Watched it disappear. His face when he turned it back to her was white and frightened. In a queer voice he asked:

'What – what was that?'

Quietly, as if to force calm upon him, she said:

'Just an aeroplane, Arthur. Such horrid, noisy things they are.'

He gazed where it had vanished, and shook his head.

'But I've *seen* an aeroplane, and *heard* it. It isn't like that. It makes a noise like a motor-bike, only louder. This was terrible! I don't understand – I don't understand what's happened . . .' His voice was pathetic.

Mrs Dolderson made as if to reply, and then checked at a thought, a sudden sharp recollection of Harold talking about dimensions, of shifting them into different planes, speaking of time as though it were simply another dimension . . . With a kind of shock of intuition she understood – no, understood was too firm a word – she perceived. But, perceiving, she found herself at a loss. She looked again at the young man. He was still tense, trembling slightly. He was wondering whether he was going out of his mind. She must stop that. There was no kind way – but how to be least unkind?

'Arthur,' she said, abruptly.

He turned a dazed look on her.

Deliberately she made her voice brisk.

'You'll find a bottle of brandy in that cupboard. Please fetch it – and two glasses,' she ordered.

With a kind of sleep-walking movement he obeyed. She filled a third of a tumbler with brandy for him, and poured a little for herself.

'Drink that,' she told him. He hesitated. 'Go on,' she commanded. 'You've had a shock. It will do you good. I want to talk to you, and I can't talk to you while you're knocked half-silly.'

He drank, coughed a little, and sat down again.

'Finish it,' she told him firmly. He finished it. Presently she inquired:

'Feeling better now?'

He nodded, but said nothing. She made up her mind, and drew breath carefully. Dropping the brisk tone altogether, she asked:

'Arthur. Tell me, what day is it today?'

'Day?' he said, in surprise. 'Why, it's Friday. It's the – er – twenty-seventh of June.'

'But the year, Arthur. What year?'

He turned his face fully towards her.

'I'm not *really* mad, you know. I know who I am, and where I am – I think . . . It's *things* that have gone wrong, not me. I can tell you—'

'What I want you to tell me, Arthur, is the year.' The peremptory note was back in her voice again.

He kept his eyes steadily on hers as he spoke.

'Nineteen-thirteen, of course,' he said.

Mrs Dolderson's gaze went back to the lawn and the flowers. She nodded gently. That was the year – and it had been a Friday; odd that she should remember that. It might well have been the twenty-seventh of June . . . But certainly a Friday in the summer of nineteen-thirteen was the day he had not come . . . All so long, long ago . . .

His voice recalled her. It was unsteady with anxiety.

'Why – why do you ask me that – about the year, I mean?'

His brow was so creased, his eyes so anxious. He was very young. Her heart ached for him. She put her thin fragile hand on his strong one again.

'I – I think I know,' he said shakily. 'It's – I don't see how, but you wouldn't have asked that unless . . . That's the queer thing that's happened, isn't it? Somehow it isn't nineteen-thirteen any longer – that's what you mean? The way the trees grew . . . that aeroplane . . . ' He stopped, staring at her with wide eyes. 'You must tell me . . . Please, please . . . What's happened to me? – Where am I now? – Where is this . . .?'

'My poor boy . . .' she murmured.

'Oh, please . . .'

The Times, with the crossword partly done, was pushed down into the chair beside her. She pulled it out half-reluctantly. Then she folded it over and held it towards him. His hand shook as he took it.

'London, Monday, the first of July,' he read. And then, in an incredulous whisper: '*Nineteen-sixty-three*!'

He lowered the page, looked at her imploringly.

She nodded twice, slowly.

They sat staring at one another without a word. Gradually, his expression changed. His brows came together, as though with pain. He looked round jerkily, his eyes darting here and there as if for an escape. Then they came back to her. He screwed them shut for a moment. Then opened them again, full of hurt – and fear.

'Oh, no – no . . .! No . . .! You're not . . . You can't be . . . You – you told me . . . You're Mrs Dolderson, aren't you? You said you were . . . You can't – you can't be – Thelma . . .?'

Mrs Dolderson said nothing. They gazed at one another. His face creased up like a small child's.

'Oh, God! Oh – oh – oh . . .!' he cried, and hid his face in his hands.

Mrs Dolderson's eyes closed for a moment. When they opened she had control of herself again. Sadly she looked on the shaking shoulders. Her thin, blue-veined left hand reached out towards the bowed head, and stroked the fair hair, gently.

Her right hand found the bell-push on the table beside her. She pressed it, and kept her finger upon it . . .

At the sound of movement her eyes opened. The venetian blind shaded the room but let in light enough for her to see Harold standing beside her bed.

'I didn't mean to wake you, Mother,' he said.

'You didn't wake me, Harold. I was dreaming, but I was not

asleep. Sit down, my dear. I want to talk to you.'

'You mustn't tire yourself, Mother. You've had a bit of a relapse, you know.'

'I dare say, but I find it more tiring to wonder than to know. I shan't keep you long.'

'Very well, Mother.' He pulled a chair close to the bedside and sat down, taking her hand in his. She looked at his face in the dimness.

'It was you who did it, wasn't it, Harold? It was that experiment of yours that brought poor Arthur here?'

'It was an accident, Mother.'

'Tell me.'

'We were trying it out. Just a preliminary test. We knew it was theoretically possible. We had shown that if we could – oh, dear, it's so difficult to explain in words – if we could, well, twist a dimension, kind of fold it back on itself, then two points that are normally apart must coincide . . . I'm afraid that's not very clear . . . '

'Never mind, dear. Go on.'

'Well, when we had our field-distortion-generator fixed up we set it to bring together two points that are normally fifty years apart. Think of folding over a long strip of paper that has two marks on it, so that the marks are brought together.'

'Yes?'

'It was quite arbitrary. We might have chosen ten years, or a hundred, but we just picked on fifty. And we got astonishingly close, too, Mother, quite remarkably close. Only a four-day calendar error in fifty years. It's staggered us. The thing we've got to do now is to find out that source of error, but if you'd asked any of us to bet—'

'Yes, dear, I'm sure it was quite wonderful. But what *happened*?'

'Oh, sorry. Well, as I said, it was an accident. We only had the thing switched on for three or four seconds – and he must

have walked slap into the field of coincidence right then. An outside
– a millions-to-one chance. I wish it had not happened, but we
couldn't possibly know . . .'

She turned her head on the pillow.

'No. You couldn't know,' she agreed. 'And then?'

'Nothing, really. We didn't know until Jenny answered your bell
to find you in a faint, and this chap, Arthur, all gone to pieces, and
sent for me.

'One of the girls helped to get you to bed. Doctor Sole arrived,
and took a look at you. Then he pumped some kind of tranquillizer
into this Arthur. The poor fellow needed it, too – one hell of a thing
to happen when all you were expecting was a game of tennis with
your best girl.

'When he'd quietened down a bit he told us who he was, and
where he'd come from. Well, there was a thing for you! Accidental
living proof at the first shot.

'But all *he* wanted, poor devil, was to get back just as soon as he
could. He was very distressed – quite a painful business. Doctor
Sole wanted to put him right under to stop him cracking altogether.
It looked that way, too – and it didn't look as if he'd be any better
when he came round again, either.

'We didn't know if we *could* send him back. Transference
"forward", to put it crudely, can be regarded as an infinite
acceleration of a natural progression, but the idea of transference
"back" is full of the most disconcerting implications once you start
thinking about it. There was quite a bit of argument, but Doctor
Sole clinched it. If there was a fair chance, he said, the chap had a
right to try, and we had an obligation to try to undo what we'd
done to him. Apart from that, if we did not try we should certainly
have to explain to someone how we came to have a raving loony on
our hands, and fifty years off course, so to speak.

'We tried to make it clear to this Arthur that we couldn't be sure that it would work in reverse – and that, anyway, there was this four-day calendar error, so at best it wouldn't be exact. I don't think he really grasped that. The poor fellow was in a wretched state; all he wanted was just a chance – any kind of chance – to get out of here. He was simply one-track.

'So we decided to take the risk – after all, if it turned out not to be possible he'd – well, he'd know nothing about it – or nothing would happen at all . . .

'The generator was still on the same setting. We put one fellow on to that, took this Arthur back to the path by your room, and got him lined up there.

'"Now walk forward," we told him. "Just as you were walking when it happened." And we gave the switch-on signal. What with the doctor's dope and one thing and another he was pretty groggy, but he did his best to pull himself together. He went forward at a kind of stagger. Literal-minded fellow; he was half-crying, but in a queer sort of voice he was trying to sing: "Everybody's doin' it, do—"

'And then he disappeared – just vanished completely.' He paused, and added regretfully: 'All the evidence we have now is not very convincing – one tennis-racket, practically new, but vintage, and one straw-hat, ditto.'

Mrs Dolderson lay without speaking. He said:

'We did our best, Mother. We could only try.'

'Of course you did, dear. And you succeeded. It wasn't your fault that you couldn't undo what you'd done . . . No, I was just wondering what would have happened if it had been a few minutes earlier – or later, that you had switched your machine on. But I don't suppose that *could* have happened . . . You wouldn't have been here at all if it had . . .'

He regarded her a little uneasily.

'What *do* you mean, Mother?'

'Never mind, dear. It was, as you said, an accident. – At least, I suppose it was – though so many important things seem to be accidents that one does sometimes wonder if they aren't really *written* somewhere . . .'

Harold looked at her, trying to make something of that, then he decided to ask:

'But what makes you think that we did succeed in getting him back, Mother?'

'Oh, I *know* you did, dear. For one thing I can very clearly remember the day I read in the paper that Lieutenant Arthur Waring Batley had been awarded a D.S.O.* – some time in November nineteen-fifteen, I think it was.

'And, for another, I have just had a letter from your sister.'

'From Cynthia? How on earth does she come into it?'

'She wants to come and see us. She is thinking of getting married again, and she'd like to bring the young man – well, not such a very *young* man, I suppose – down here to show him.'

'That's all right, but I don't see—'

'She thinks you might find him interesting. He's a physicist.'

'But—'

Mrs Dolderson took no notice of the interruption. She went on:

'Cynthia tells me his name is Batley – and he's the son of a Colonel Arthur Waring Batley, D.S.O., of Nairobi, Kenya.'

'You mean, he's the son of . . .?'

'So it would seem, dear. Strange, isn't it?' She reflected a moment, and added: 'I must say that if these things *are* written, they do sometimes seem to be written in a very queerly distorted way, don't you think . . .?'

NOTES

D.S.O. (p119)
Distinguished Service Order; a medal won for bravery in war

DISCUSSION

1 Do you think the shock of the meeting was worse for Thelma or for Arthur? Why? If it had happened to you, whose position would you rather have been in?

2 After he had been sent back to his own time, why do you think Arthur never got in touch with Thelma again?

3 What is your opinion of the coincidence of Arthur's son and Thelma's daughter meeting and falling in love? Would you have preferred another ending to the story? If so, what?

4 'What a curious, haphazard thing one's existence was.' (p107) Do you agree with this view, or do you believe our destinies are already planned or 'written', and no decision or action on our parts can change them?

LANGUAGE FOCUS

1 Find these expressions in the text and rephrase them in your own words.

> *to keep the house up* (p105)
> *one gave up trying to understand* (p105)
> *Last time the subject had cropped up* (p106)
> *Strange, it was, the way things fell out.* (p106)
> *He did his best to pull himself together* (p109)
> *He broke off* (p110)
> *to put him right under* (p117)
> *if it turned out not to be possible* (p118)

2 The title of the story echoes the English proverb 'A stitch in time saves nine'. Write down what you think is the literal meaning of this proverb, and then an explanation of the figurative meaning. Think of some specific situations that you could apply this proverb to. Do you think it applies to this story? If so, in what way? If not, what do you think the author meant by 'stitch in time'?

ACTIVITIES

1   Write Arthur's diary for the day he travelled fifty years. Does he accept the idea of time-travel, do you think, or does he explain events to himself in a different way?

2   Imagine that Arthur comes to England for the wedding of his son to Thelma's daughter Cynthia, and so meets Thelma again. What might they say to each other? Write down their conversation.

3   Suppose that one of your ancestors from a hundred years ago travelled into the present age for a week's visit. What inventions or customs or attitudes of the modern age do you think she or he would find most shocking and alarming? Choose three or four things and write some notes to explain them in a way that your ancestor might understand.

THE SOUND MACHINE

THE AUTHOR

Roald Dahl was born in Wales in 1916 of Norwegian parents. He served as a fighter pilot in World War II, and his first volume of short stories, *Over to You*, was based on his wartime experiences. Other collections are *Kiss Kiss, Someone Like You, Switch Bitch*, and *Further Tales of the Unexpected*; they have been translated into many languages and are bestsellers all over the world. His stories, bizarre and alarming, often with a touch of black humour, are more in the fantasy and horror genres but sometimes make use of science-fiction images. His stories for children, such as *Charlie and the Chocolate Factory*, are also enormously popular. He died in 1990.

THE STORY

It is hard to escape from sound of one kind or another – traffic, birdsong, voices, the soft thump of one's heartbeat at night. There are those who claim to hear sounds inaudible to others – the voice of God, for example. Is this just the product of some chemical malfunction in the brain? Human ears cannot hear the high-pitched squeak of a bat, but does that mean it does not exist? 'I am too much of a sceptic,' wrote the English biologist T. H. Huxley, 'to deny the possibility of anything.'

In a garden shed in a quiet suburb Klausner bends over his workbench, intent, absorbed, his hands busily adjusting wires inside a long black box. He is interrupted by a visitor, Dr Scott, calling to enquire after his sore throat. Klausner answers briefly, dismissively, but the Doctor lingers, curious to know the purpose of that strange black box . . .

THE SOUND MACHINE

It was a warm summer evening and Klausner walked quickly through the front gate and around the side of the house and into the garden at the back. He went on down the garden until he came to a wooden shed and he unlocked the door, went inside and closed the door behind him.

The interior of the shed was an unpainted room. Against one wall, on the left, there was a long wooden workbench, and on it, among a littering of wires and batteries and small sharp tools, there stood a black box about three feet long, the shape of a child's coffin.

Klausner moved across the room to the box. The top of the box was open, and he bent down and began to poke and peer inside it among a mass of different-coloured wires and silver tubes. He picked up a piece of paper that lay beside the box, studied it carefully, put it down, peered inside the box and started running his fingers along the wires, tugging gently at them to test the connections, glancing back at the paper, then into the box, then at the paper again, checking each wire. He did this for perhaps an hour.

Then he put a hand around to the front of the box where there were three dials, and he began to twiddle them, watching at the same time the movement of the mechanism inside the box. All the while he kept speaking softly to himself, nodding his head, smiling sometimes, his hands always moving, the fingers moving swiftly, deftly, inside the box, his mouth twisting into curious shapes when a thing was delicate or difficult to do, saying, 'Yes . . . Yes . . . And now this one . . . Yes . . . Yes. But is this right? Is it – where's my diagram? . . . Ah, yes . . . Of course . . . Yes, yes . . . That's right . . . And now . . . Good . . . Good . . . Yes . . . Yes, yes, yes.' His concentration was intense; his movements were quick; there was an air of urgency about the way he worked, of breathlessness, of strong suppressed excitement.

Suddenly he heard footsteps on the gravel path outside and he straightened and turned swiftly as the door opened and a tall man came in. It was Scott. It was only Scott, the doctor.

'Well, well, well,' the Doctor said. 'So this is where you hide yourself in the evenings.'

'Hullo, Scott,' Klausner said.

'I happened to be passing,' the Doctor told him, 'so I dropped in to see how you were. There was no one in the house, so I came on down here. How's that throat of yours been behaving?'

'It's all right. It's fine.'

'Now I'm here I might as well have a look at it.'

'Please don't trouble. I'm quite cured. I'm fine.'

The Doctor began to feel the tension in the room. He looked at the black box on the bench; then he looked at the man. 'You've got your hat on,' he said.

'Oh, have I?' Klausner reached up, removed the hat, and put it on the bench.

The Doctor came up closer and bent down to look into the box. 'What's this?' he said. 'Making a radio?'

'No, just fooling around.'

'It's got rather complicated-looking innards.'

'Yes.' Klausner seemed tense and distracted.

'What is it?' the Doctor asked. 'It's rather a frightening-looking thing, isn't it?'

'It's just an idea.'

'Yes?'

'It has to do with sound, that's all.'

'Good heavens, man! Don't you get enough of that sort of thing all day in your work?'

'I like sound.'

'So it seems.' The Doctor went to the door, turned, and said, 'Well, I won't disturb you. Glad your throat's not worrying you any more.' But he kept standing there looking at the box, intrigued by the remarkable complexity of its inside, curious to know what this strange patient of his was up to. 'What's it really for?' he asked. 'You've made me inquisitive.'

Klausner looked down at the box, then at the Doctor, and he reached up and began gently to scratch the lobe of his right ear. There was a pause. The Doctor stood by the door, waiting, smiling.

'All right, I'll tell you, if you're interested.' There was another pause, and the Doctor could see that Klausner was having trouble about how to begin.

He was shifting from one foot to the other, tugging at the lobe of his ear, looking at his feet, and then at last, slowly, he said, 'Well, it's like this . . . the theory is very simple really. The human ear . . . you know that it can't hear everything. There are sounds that are so low-pitched or so high-pitched that it can't hear them.'

'Yes,' the Doctor said. 'Yes.'

'Well, speaking very roughly, any note so high that it has more than fifteen thousand vibrations a second – we can't hear it. Dogs have better ears than us. You know you can buy a whistle whose note is so high-pitched that you can't hear it at all. But a dog can hear it.'

'Yes, I've seen one,' the Doctor said.

'Of course you have. And up the scale, higher than the note of that whistle, there is another note – a vibration if you like, but I prefer to think of it as a note. You can't hear that one either. And above that there is another and another rising right up the scale for ever and ever and ever, an endless succession of notes . . . an infinity of notes . . . there is a note – if only our ears could hear it – so high that it vibrates a million times a second . . . and another a million times as high as that . . . and on and on, higher and higher, as far as numbers go, which is . . . infinity . . . eternity . . . beyond the stars.'

Klausner was becoming more animated every moment. He was a small frail man, nervous and twitchy, with always moving hands. His large head inclined towards his left shoulder as though his neck were not quite strong enough to support it rigidly. His face was smooth and pale, almost white, and the pale-grey eyes that blinked and peered from behind a pair of steel spectacles were bewildered, unfocused, remote. He was a frail, nervous, twitchy little man, a moth of a man, dreamy and distracted; suddenly fluttering and animated; and now the Doctor, looking at that strange pale face and those pale-grey eyes, felt that somehow there was about this little person a quality of distance, of immense immeasurable distance, as though the mind were far away from where the body was.

The Doctor waited for him to go on. Klausner sighed and clasped his hands tightly together. 'I believe,' he said, speaking more slowly now, 'that there is a whole world of sound about us all the time that we cannot hear. It is possible that up there in those high-pitched inaudible regions there is a new exciting music being made, with subtle harmonies and fierce grinding discords, a music so powerful that it would drive us mad if only our ears were tuned to hear the sound of it. There may be anything . . . for all we know there may—'

'Yes,' the Doctor said. 'But it's not very probable.'

'Why not? Why not?' Klausner pointed to a fly sitting on a small roll of copper wire on the workbench. 'You see that fly? What sort of a noise is that fly making now? None – that one can hear. But for all we know the creature may be whistling like mad on a very high note, or barking or croaking or singing a song. It's got a mouth, hasn't it? It's got a throat!'

The Doctor looked at the fly and he smiled. He was still standing by the door with his hands on the doorknob. 'Well,' he said. 'So you're going to check up on that?'

'Some time ago,' Klausner said, 'I made a simple instrument that proved to me the existence of many odd inaudible sounds. Often I have sat and watched the needle of my instrument recording the presence of sound vibrations in the air when I myself could hear nothing. And *those* are the sounds I want to listen to. I want to know where they come from and who or what is making them.'

'And that machine on the table there,' the Doctor said, 'is that going to allow you to hear these noises?'

'It may. Who knows? So far, I've had no luck. But I've made some changes in it and tonight I'm ready for another trial. This machine,' he said, touching it with his hands, 'is designed to pick up sound vibrations that are too high-pitched for reception by the human ear, and to convert them to a scale of audible tones. I tune it in, almost like a radio.'

'How d'you mean?'

'It isn't complicated. Say I wish to listen to the squeak of a bat. That's a fairly high-pitched sound – about thirty thousand vibrations a second. The average human ear can't quite hear it. Now, if there were a bat flying around this room and I tuned in to thirty thousand on my machine, I would hear the squeaking of that bat very clear. I would even hear the correct note – F sharp, or B flat, or whatever it might be – but merely at a much *lower pitch*. Don't you understand?'

The Doctor looked at the long, black coffin-box. 'And you're going to try it tonight?'

'Yes.'

'Well, I wish you luck.' He glanced at his watch. 'My goodness!' he said. 'I must fly. Goodbye, and thank you for telling me. I must call again some time and find out what happened.' The Doctor went out and closed the door behind him.

For a while longer, Klausner fussed about with the wires in the black box; then he straightened up and in a soft excited whisper said, 'Now we'll try again . . . We'll take it out into the garden this time . . . and then perhaps . . . perhaps . . . the reception will be better. Lift it up now . . . carefully . . . Oh, my God, it's heavy!' He carried the box to the door, found that he couldn't open the door without putting it down, carried it back, put it on the bench, opened the door, and then carried it with some difficulty into the garden. He placed the box carefully on a small wooden table that stood on the lawn. He returned to the shed and fetched a pair of earphones. He plugged the wire connections from the earphones into the machine and put the earphones over his ears. The movements of his hands were quick and precise. He was excited, and breathed loudly and quickly through his mouth. He kept on talking to himself with little words of comfort and encouragement, as though he were afraid – afraid that the machine might not work and afraid also of what might happen if it did.

He stood there in the garden beside the wooden table, so pale, small, and thin that he looked like an ancient, consumptive, bespectacled child. The sun had gone down. There was no wind, no sound at all. From where he stood, he could see over a low fence into the next garden, and there was a woman walking down the garden with a flower-basket on her arm. He watched her for a while without thinking about her at all. Then he turned to the box on the table and pressed a switch on its front. He put his left hand on the volume control and his right hand on the knob that moved a needle across a large central dial, like the wavelength dial of a radio. The dial was marked with many numbers, in a series of bands, starting at 15,000 and going on up to 1,000,000.

And now he was bending forward over the machine. His head was cocked to one side in a tense, listening attitude. His right hand was beginning to turn the knob. The needle was travelling slowly across the dial, so slowly he could hardly see it move, and in the earphones he could hear a faint, spasmodic crackling.

Behind this crackling sound he could hear a distant humming tone which was the noise of the machine itself, but that was all. As he listened, he became conscious of a curious sensation, a feeling that his ears were stretching out away from his head, that each ear was connected to his head by a thin stiff wire, like a tentacle, and that the wires were lengthening, that the ears were going up and up towards a secret and forbidden territory, a dangerous ultrasonic region where ears had never been before and had no right to be.

The little needle crept slowly across the dial, and suddenly he heard a shriek, a frightful piercing shriek, and he jumped and dropped his hands, catching hold of the edge of the table. He stared around him as if expecting to see the person who had shrieked. There was no one in sight except the woman in the garden next door, and it was certainly not she. She was bending down, cutting yellow roses and putting them in her basket.

Again it came – a throatless, inhuman shriek, sharp and short, very clear and cold. The note itself possessed a minor, metallic quality that he had never heard before. Klausner looked around him, searching instinctively for the source of the noise. The woman next door was the only living thing in sight. He saw her reach down, take a rose stem in the fingers of one hand and snip the stem with a pair of scissors. Again he heard the scream.

It came at the exact moment when the rose stem was cut.

At this point, the woman straightened up, put the scissors in the basket with the roses, and turned to walk away.

'Mrs Saunders!' Klausner shouted, his voice shrill with excitement. 'Oh, Mrs Saunders!'

And looking round, the woman saw her neighbour standing on his lawn – a fantastic, arm-waving little person with a pair of earphones on his head – calling to her in a voice so high and loud that she became alarmed.

'Cut another one! Please cut another one quickly!'

She stood still, staring at him. 'Why, Mr Klausner,' she said. 'What's the matter?'

'Please do as I ask,' he said. 'Cut just one more rose!'

Mrs Saunders had always believed her neighbour to be a rather peculiar person; now it seemed that he had gone completely crazy. She wondered whether she should run into the house and fetch her husband. No, she thought. No, he's harmless. I'll just humour him. 'Certainly, Mr Klausner, if you like,' she said. She took her scissors from the basket, bent down, and snipped another rose.

Again Klausner heard that frightful, throatless shriek in the earphones; again it came at the exact moment the rose stem was cut. He took off the earphones and ran to the fence that separated the two gardens. 'All right,' he said. 'That's enough. No more. Please, no more.'

The woman stood there, a yellow rose in one hand, clippers in the other, looking at him.

'I'm going to tell you something, Mrs Saunders,' he said, 'something that you won't believe.' He put his hands on top of the fence and peered at her intently through his thick spectacles. 'You have, this evening, cut a basketful of roses. You have with a sharp pair of scissors cut through the stems of living things, and each rose that you cut screamed in the most terrible way. Did you know that, Mrs Saunders?'

'No,' she said. 'I certainly didn't know that.'

'It happens to be true,' he said. He was breathing rather rapidly, but he was trying to control his excitement. 'I heard them shrieking. Each time you cut one, I heard the cry of pain. A very high-pitched sound, approximately one hundred and thirty-two thousand vibrations a second. You couldn't possibly have heard it yourself. But *I* heard it.'

'Did you really, Mr Klausner?' She decided she would make a dash for the house in about five seconds.

'You might say,' he went on, 'that a rose bush has no nervous system to feel with, no throat to cry with. You'd be right. It hasn't. Not like ours, anyway. But *how do you know, Mrs Saunders*' – and here he leaned far over the fence and spoke in a fierce whisper – '*how do you know* that a rose bush doesn't feel as much pain when someone cuts its stem in two as you would feel if someone cut your wrist off with a garden shears? *How do you know that*? It's *alive*, isn't it?'

'Yes, Mr Klausner. Oh, yes – and goodnight.' Quickly she turned and ran up the garden to her house. Klausner went back to the table. He put on the earphones and stood for a while listening. He could still hear the faint crackling sound and the humming noise of the machine, but nothing more. He bent down and took hold of a small white daisy growing on the lawn. He took it between thumb and forefinger and slowly pulled it upward and sideways until the stem broke.

From the moment that he started pulling to the moment when the stem broke, he heard – he distinctly heard in the earphones – a faint high-pitched cry, curiously inanimate. He took another daisy and did it again. Once more he heard the cry, but he wasn't so sure now that it expressed *pain*. No, it wasn't pain, it was surprise. Or was it? It didn't really express any of the feelings or emotions known to a human being. It was just a cry, a neutral, stony cry – a single emotionless note, expressing nothing. It had been the same with the roses. He had been wrong in calling it a cry of pain. A flower probably didn't feel pain. It felt something else which we didn't know about – something called toin or spurl or plinuckment*, or anything you like.

He stood up and removed the earphones. It was getting dark and he could see pricks of light shining in the windows of the houses all around him. Carefully he picked up the black box from the table, carried it into the shed and put it on the workbench. Then he went out, locked the door behind him, and walked up to the house.

The next morning Klausner was up as soon as it was light. He dressed and went straight to the shed. He picked up the machine and carried it outside, clasping it to his chest with both hands, walking unsteadily under its weight. He went past the house, out through the front gate, and across the road to the park. There he paused and looked around him; then he went on until he came to a large tree, a beech tree, and he placed the machine on the ground close to the trunk of the tree. Quickly he went back to the house and got an axe from the coal cellar and carried it across the road into the park. He put the axe on the ground beside the tree.

Then he looked around him again, peering nervously through his thick glasses in every direction. There was no one about. It was six in the morning.

He put the earphones on his head and switched on the machine. He listened for a moment to the faint familiar humming sound; then he picked up the axe, took a stance with his legs wide apart, and swung the axe as hard as he could at the base of the tree trunk. The blade cut deep into the wood and stuck there, and at the instant of impact he heard a most extraordinary noise in the earphones. It was a new noise, unlike any he had heard before – a harsh, noteless, enormous noise, a growling, low-pitched, screaming sound, not quick and short like the noise of the roses, but drawn out like a sob lasting for fully a minute, loudest at the moment when the axe struck, fading gradually fainter and fainter until it was gone.

Klausner stared in horror at the place where the blade of the axe had sunk into the woodflesh of the tree; then gently he took the axe handle, worked the blade loose and threw the thing to the ground. With his fingers he touched the gash that the axe had made in the wood, touching the edges of the gash, trying to press them together to close the wound, and he kept saying, 'Tree . . . oh, tree . . . I am sorry . . . I am so sorry . . . but it will heal . . . it will heal fine . . . '

For a while he stood there with his hands upon the trunk of the great tree; then suddenly he turned away and hurried off out of the park, across the road, through the front gate and back into his house. He went to the telephone, consulted the book, dialled a number and waited. He held the receiver tightly in his left hand and tapped the table impatiently with his right. He heard the telephone buzzing at the other end, and then the click of a lifted receiver and a man's voice, a sleepy voice, saying: 'Hullo. Yes.'

'Dr Scott?' he said.

'Yes. Speaking.'

'Dr Scott. You must come at once – quickly, please.'

'Who is it speaking?'

'Klausner here, and you remember what I told you last night about my experience with sound, and how I hoped I might—'

'Yes, yes, of course, but what's the matter? Are you ill?'

'No, I'm not ill, but—'

'It's half-past six in the morning,' the Doctor said, 'and you call me but you are not ill.'

'Please come. Come quickly. I want someone to hear it. It's driving me mad! I can't believe it . . .'

The Doctor heard the frantic, almost hysterical note in the man's voice, the same note he was used to hearing in the voices of people who called up and said, 'There's been an accident. Come quickly.' He said slowly, 'You really want me to get out of bed and come over now?'

'Yes, now. At once, please.'

'All right, then – I'll come.'

Klausner sat down beside the telephone and waited. He tried to remember what the shriek of the tree had sounded like, but he couldn't. He could remember only that it had been enormous and frightful and that it had made him feel sick with horror. He tried to imagine what sort of noise a human would make if he had to stand anchored to the ground while someone deliberately swung a small sharp thing at his leg so that the blade cut in deep and wedged itself in the cut. Same sort of noise perhaps? No. Quite different. The noise of the tree was worse than any known human noise because of that frightening, toneless, throatless quality. He began to wonder about other living things, and he thought immediately of a field of wheat, a field of wheat standing up straight and yellow and alive, with the mower going through it, cutting the stems, five hundred stems a second, every second. Oh, my God, what would *that* noise be like? Five hundred wheat plants screaming together and every second another five hundred being cut and screaming and – no, he thought, I do not want to go to a wheat field with my machine. I would never eat bread after that. But what about potatoes and cabbages and carrots and onions? And what about apples? Ah, no. Apples are all right. They fall off naturally when they are ripe. Apples are all right if you let them fall off instead of tearing them from the tree branch. But not vegetables. Not a potato for example. A potato would surely shriek; so would a carrot and an onion and a cabbage . . .

He heard the click of the front-gate latch and he jumped up and went out and saw the tall doctor coming down the path, little black bag in hand.

'Well,' the Doctor said. 'Well, what's all the trouble?'

'Come with me, Doctor. I want you to hear it. I called you because you're the only one I've told. It's over the road in the park. Will you come now?'

The Doctor looked at him. He seemed calmer now. There was no sign of madness or hysteria, he was merely disturbed and excited.

They went across the road into the park and Klausner led the way to the great beech tree at the foot of which stood the long black coffin-box of the machine – and the axe.

'Why did you bring it out here?' the Doctor asked.

'I wanted a tree. There aren't any big trees in the garden.'

'And why the axe?'

'You'll see in a moment. But now please put on these earphones and listen. Listen carefully and tell me afterwards precisely what you hear. I want to make quite sure . . .'

The Doctor smiled and took the earphones and put them over his ears.

Klausner bent down and flicked the switch on the panel of the machine, then he picked up the axe and took his stance with his legs apart, ready to swing. For a moment he paused.

'Can you hear anything?' he said to the Doctor.

'Can I what?'

'Can you *hear* anything?'

'Just a humming noise.'

Klausner stood there with the axe in his hands trying to bring himself to swing, but the thought of the noise that the tree would make made him pause again.

'What are you waiting for?' the Doctor asked.

'Nothing,' Klausner answered, and then he lifted the axe and swung it at the tree, and as he swung, he thought he felt, he could swear he felt a movement of the ground on which he stood. He felt a slight shifting of the earth beneath his feet as though the roots of the tree were moving underneath the soil, but it was too late to check the blow and the axe blade struck the tree and wedged deep into the wood. At that moment, high overhead, there was the cracking sound of wood splintering and the swishing sound of leaves brushing against other leaves and they both looked up and the Doctor cried, 'Watch out! Run, man! Quickly, run!'

The Doctor had ripped off the earphones and was running away fast, but Klausner stood spellbound, staring up at the great branch, sixty feet long at least, that was bending slowly downward, breaking and crackling and splintering at its thickest point, where it joined the main trunk of the tree. The branch came crashing down and Klausner leapt aside just in time. It fell upon the machine and smashed it into pieces.

'Great heavens!' shouted the Doctor as he came running back. 'That was a near one! I thought it had got you!'

Klausner was staring at the tree. His large head was leaning to one side and upon his smooth white face there was a tense, horrified expression. Slowly he walked up to the tree and gently he prised the blade loose from the trunk.

'Did you hear it?' he said, turning to the Doctor. His voice was barely audible.

The Doctor was still out of breath from running and the excitement. 'Hear what?'

'In the earphones. Did you hear anything when the axe struck?'

The Doctor began to rub the back of his neck. 'Well,' he said, 'as a matter of fact . . .' He paused and frowned and bit his lower lip. 'No, I'm not sure. I couldn't be sure. I don't suppose I had the earphones on for more than a second after the axe struck.'

'Yes, yes, but what did you hear?'

'I don't know,' the Doctor said. 'I don't know what I heard. Probably the noise of the branch breaking.' He was speaking rapidly, rather irritably.

'What did it sound like?' Klausner leaned forward slightly, staring hard at the Doctor. '*Exactly* what did it sound like?'

'Oh, hell!' the Doctor said. 'I really don't know. I was more interested in getting out of the way. Let's leave it.'

'Dr Scott, *what-did-it-sound-like?*'

'For God's sake, how could I tell, what with half the tree falling on me and having to run for my life?' The Doctor certainly seemed nervous. Klausner had sensed it now. He stood quite still, staring at the Doctor and for fully half a minute he didn't speak. The Doctor moved his feet, shrugged his shoulders and half turned to go. 'Well,' he said, 'we'd better get back.'

'Look,' said the little man, and now his smooth white face became suddenly suffused with colour. 'Look,' he said, 'you stitch this up.' He pointed to the last gash that the axe had made in the tree trunk. 'You stitch this up quickly.'

'Don't be silly,' the Doctor said.

'You do as I say. Stitch it up.' Klausner was gripping the axe handle and he spoke softly, in a curious, almost a threatening tone.

'Don't be silly,' the Doctor said. 'I can't stitch through wood. Come on. Let's get back.'

'So you can't stitch through wood?'

'No, of course not.'

'Have you got any iodine in your bag?'

'What if I have?'

'Then paint the cut with iodine. It'll sting, but that can't be helped.'

'Now look,' the Doctor said, and again he turned as if to go. 'Let's not be ridiculous. Let's get back to the house and then . . .'

'*Paint-the-cut-with-iodine.*'

The Doctor hesitated. He saw Klausner's hands tightening on the handle of the axe. He decided that his only alternative was to run away fast, and he certainly wasn't going to do that.

'All right,' he said. 'I'll paint it with iodine.'

He got his black bag which was lying on the grass about ten yards away, opened it and took out a bottle of iodine and some cotton wool. He went up to the tree trunk, uncorked the bottle, tipped some of the iodine on to the cotton wool, bent down, and began to dab it into the cut. He kept one eye on Klausner who was standing motionless with the axe in his hands, watching him.

'Make sure you get it right in.'

'Yes,' the Doctor said.

'Now do the other one – the one just above it!'

The Doctor did as he was told.

'There you are,' he said. 'It's done.'

He straightened up and surveyed his work in a very serious manner. 'That should do nicely.'

Klausner came closer and gravely examined the two wounds.

'Yes,' he said, nodding his huge head slowly up and down. 'Yes, that will do nicely.' He stepped back a pace. 'You'll come and look at them again tomorrow?'

'Oh, yes,' the Doctor said. 'Of course.'

'And put some more iodine on?'

'If necessary, yes.'

'Thank you, Doctor,' Klausner said, and he nodded his head again and he dropped the axe and all at once he smiled, a wild, excited smile, and quickly the Doctor went over to him and gently he took him by the arm and he said, 'Come on, we must go now,' and suddenly they were walking away, the two of them, walking silently, rather hurriedly across the park, over the road, back to the house.

NOTES

toin, spurl, plinuckment (p131)
  words invented by the author

DISCUSSION

1 Describe Mrs Saunders' and the Doctor's reactions to Klausner's theory. Are they the same? Why does the Doctor seem uneasy when Klausner questions him about the sound the tree made?

2 How do you interpret the branch breaking off and crashing down to destroy the sound machine – as a coincidence, or as something more sinister? How do you think Klausner and the doctor interpret this event?

3 How likely is it, do you think, that plants when damaged make sounds inaudible to human ears? On a scale of probability from 1 to 10, with 1 being impossible and 10 being quite possible, where would you place the idea? What reasons would you give to support your opinion?

LANGUAGE FOCUS

1 Find all the vocabulary and expressions in the story used to describe Klausner's actions and behaviour that suggest to you he is, if not mad, at least very close to it.

2 Find the two speeches where Klausner is talking about the fly to the Doctor, and the rose bush to Mrs Saunders:

   • 'You see that fly? . . . . . It's got a throat!' (p126)

   • 'You might say that a rose bush . . . . . It's alive, isn't it?' (p131)

   Klausner is speaking in a very excitable, assertive way in these two speeches. Rewrite both of them, in a much more cautious, reasonable way, trying to persuade the listeners that these are ideas worth taking seriously.

3 The last sentence of the story consists of several clauses, all joined by the same conjunction 'and'. What is the effect of this rather unusual style? Try rewriting the paragraph in shorter sentences, using different linking words and participles. Does your sentence have the same effect as the original one? Which do you think suits the story better, and why?

ACTIVITIES

1 Imagine that you are a journalist for the local newspaper in the town where Klausner lives. The smashed sound machine is found in the park by the police, who trace it to Klausner. After interviewing Dr Scott, Mrs Saunders, and Klausner himself, write your report for the newspaper. You could take a line sympathetic to Klausner's theory, or sceptical, or ridiculing.

2 Did you feel the ending of the story was inconclusive? What do you think happened to Klausner? Did he build another sound machine and prove to the world that his theory was correct? Did he starve himself to death because he could not bring himself to eat any plants? Write another paragraph as an epilogue to the story, describing Klausner ten years later.

3 After Klausner's experiences with the sound machine, he feels that, like vegetarians with regard to meat, he cannot inflict 'pain' on living plants. What else, besides apples, would he feel able to eat? In what other ways would life be difficult for him: for example, could he wear clothing made of cotton or silk, or use furniture made of wood? Write a list of the items that you think he would feel able to use.

THE HAMMER OF GOD

THE AUTHOR

Arthur C. Clarke was born in 1917 in Somerset, England, and since 1956 has lived in Sri Lanka. With a degree in physics and mathematics, he has been a great popularizer of science (publishing plans for communications satellites well before they became reality), as well a famous writer of science fiction. His writing combines metaphysical themes with ardent support for technological progress and space exploration. Among his many well-known works are *Childhood's End, The City and the Stars, Rendezvous with Rama*, and the collaboration with Stanley Kubrick on the film *2001: A Space Odyssey. The Hammer of God*, first published in 1992 in *Time* magazine, has since appeared in a full-length novel version and there are plans for a film.

THE STORY

On 30 June 1908 a small asteroid entered the Earth's atmosphere and exploded 10km above the Tunguska forests of Siberia. The explosion, a thousand times larger than the Hiroshima bomb, could be seen 500km away and felt all around the world. The blast flattened 2000 square kilometres of forest, caused widespread fires, and left a thick pall of dust hanging in the air. An impact such as this, or worse, could happen again any day – or not for another several thousand years.

It has been many decades since Captain Robert Singh set foot on Earth. He can call up memories, of course, at the touch of a button and relive all the sights, sounds, and scents of his past. But for now, he has a job to do. Sighing a little, he turns to the viewport of his spacecraft and sees Kali, hanging harmlessly in the blackness of space – Kali, the hammer of God . . .

THE HAMMER OF GOD

It came in vertically, punching a hole 10 km wide through the atmosphere, generating temperatures so high that the air itself started to burn. When it hit the ground near the Gulf of Mexico, rock turned to liquid and spread outward in mountainous waves, not freezing until it had formed a crater 200 km across.

That was only the beginning of disaster: now the real tragedy began. Nitric oxides rained from the air, turning the sea to acid. Clouds of soot from incinerated forests darkened the sky, hiding the sun for months. Worldwide, the temperature dropped precipitously, killing off most of the plants and animals that had survived the initial cataclysm. Though some species would linger on for millenniums, the reign of the great reptiles was finally over.

The clock of evolution had been reset; the countdown to Man had begun. The date was, very approximately, 65 million BC.

Captain Robert Singh never tired of walking in the forest with his little son Toby. It was, of course, a tamed and gentle forest, guaranteed to be free of dangerous animals, but it made an exciting contrast to the rolling sand dunes of their last environment in the Saudi desert – and the one before that, on Australia's Great Barrier Reef. But when the Skylift Service had moved the house this time, something had gone wrong with the food-recycling system. Though the electronic menus had fail-safe backups, there had been a curious metallic taste to some of the items coming out of the synthesizer recently.

'What's that, Daddy?' asked the four-year-old, pointing to a small hairy face peering at them through a screen of leaves.

'Er, some kind of monkey. We'll ask the Brain when we get home.'

'Can I play with it?'

'I don't think that's a good idea. It could bite. And it probably has fleas. Your robotoys are much nicer.'

'But . . .'

Captain Singh knew what would happen next: he had run this sequence a dozen times. Toby would begin to cry, the monkey would disappear, he would comfort the child as he carried him back to the house . . .

But that had been twenty years ago and a quarter-billion kilometers away. The playback came to an end; sound, vision, the scent of unknown flowers and the gentle touch of the wind slowly faded. Suddenly, he was back in this cabin aboard the orbital tug *Goliath*, commanding the 100-person team of Operation ATLAS, the most critical mission in the history of space exploration. Toby, and the stepmothers and stepfathers of his extended family, remained behind on a distant world which Singh could never revisit. Decades in space – and neglect of the mandatory zero-G* exercises – had so weakened him that he could now walk only on the Moon and Mars. Gravity had exiled him from the planet of his birth.

'One hour to rendezvous, captain,' said the quiet but insistent voice of David*, as *Goliath*'s central computer had been inevitably named. 'Active mode, as requested. Time to come back to the real world.'

Goliath's human commander felt a wave of sadness sweep over him as the final image from his lost past dissolved into a featureless, simmering mist of white noise. Too swift a transition from one reality to another was a good recipe for schizophrenia, and Captain Singh always eased the shock with the most soothing sound he knew: waves falling gently on a beach, with sea gulls crying in the distance. It was yet another memory of a life he had lost, and of a peaceful past that had now been replaced by a fearful present.

For a few more moments, he delayed facing his awesome responsibility. Then he sighed and removed the neural-input cap that fitted snugly over his skull and had enabled him to call up his distant past. Like all spacers, Captain Singh belonged to the 'Bald Is Beautiful' school, if only because wigs were a nuisance in zero gravity. The social historians were still staggered by the fact that one invention, the portable 'Brainman', could make bare heads the norm within a single decade. Not even quick-change skin coloring, or the lens-corrective laser shaping which had abolished eyeglasses, had made such an impact upon style and fashion.

'Captain,' said David. 'I know you're there. Or do you want me to take over?'

It was an old joke, inspired by all the insane computers in the fiction and movies of the early electronic age. David had a surprisingly good sense of humor: he was, after all, a Legal Person (Nonhuman) under the famous Hundredth Amendment, and shared – or surpassed – almost all the attributes of his creators. But there were whole sensory and emotional areas which he could not enter. It had been felt unnecessary to equip him with smell or taste, though it would have been easy to do so. And all his attempts at telling dirty stories were such disastrous failures that he had abandoned the genre.

'All right, David,' replied the captain. 'I'm still in charge.' He removed the mask from his eyes, and turned reluctantly toward the viewport. There, hanging in space before him, was Kali*.

It looked harmless enough: just another small asteroid, shaped so exactly like a peanut that the resemblance was almost comical. A few large impact craters, and hundreds of tiny ones, were scattered at random over its charcoal-gray surface. There were no visual clues to give any sense of scale, but Singh knew its dimensions by heart: 1,295m maximum length, 456m minimum width. Kali would fit easily into many city parks.

No wonder that, even now, most of humankind could still not believe that this modest asteroid was the instrument of doom. Or, as the Chrislamic Fundamentalists were calling it, 'the Hammer of God'.

• • •

The sudden rise of Chrislam* had been traumatic equally to Rome and Mecca. Christianity was already reeling from John Paul XXV's eloquent but belated plea for contraception and the irrefutable proof in the New Dead Sea Scrolls* that the Jesus of the Gospels was a composite of at least three persons. Meanwhile the Muslim world had lost much of its economic power when the Cold Fusion* breakthrough, after the fiasco of its premature announcement, had brought the Oil Age to a sudden end. The time had been ripe for a new religion embodying, as even its severest critics admitted, the best elements of two ancient ones.

The Prophet Fatima Magdalene (née Ruby Goldenburg) had attracted almost 100 million adherents before her spectacular – and, some maintained, self-contrived – martyrdom. Thanks to the brilliant use of neural programming to give previews of Paradise during its ceremonies, Chrislam had grown explosively, though it was still far outnumbered by its parent religions.

Inevitably, after the Prophet's death the movement split into rival factions, each upholding *the* True Faith. The most fanatical was a fundamentalist group calling itself 'the Reborn', which claimed to be in direct contact with God (or at least Her Archangels) via the listening post they had established in the silent zone on the far side of the Moon, shielded from the radio racket of Earth by 3,000km of solid rock.

• • •

Now Kali filled the main viewscreen. No magnification was needed, for *Goliath* was hovering only 200m above its ancient, battered surface. Two crew members had already landed, with the traditional 'One small step for a man'* – even though walking was impossible on this almost zero-gravity worldlet.

'Deploying radio beacon. We've got it anchored securely. Now Kali won't be able to hide from us.'

It was a feeble joke, not meriting the laughter it aroused from the dozen officers on the bridge. Ever since rendezvous, there had been a subtle change in the crew's morale, with unpredictable swings between gloom and juvenile humor. The ship's physician had already prescribed tranquilizers for one mild case of manic-depressive symptoms. It would grow worse in the long weeks ahead, when there would be little to do but wait.

The first waiting period had already begun. Back on Earth, giant radio telescopes were tuned to receive the pulses from the beacon. Although Kali's orbit had already been calculated with the greatest possible accuracy, there was still a slim chance that the asteroid might pass harmlessly by. The radio measuring rod would settle the matter, for better or worse.

It was a long two hours before the verdict came, and David relayed it to the crew.

'Spaceguard reports that the probability of impact on Earth is 99.9%. Operation ATLAS will begin immediately.'

The task of the mythological Atlas was to hold up the heavens and prevent them from crashing down upon Earth. The ATLAS booster that *Goliath* carried as an external payload had a more modest goal: keeping at bay only a small piece of the sky.

* * *

It was the size of a small house, weighed 9,000 tons and was moving at 50,000 km/h. As it passed over the grand Teton National Park, one alert tourist photographed the incandescent fireball and its long vapor trail. In less than two minutes, it had sliced through the Earth's atmosphere and returned to space.

The slightest change of orbit during the billions of years it had been circling the sun might have sent the asteroid crashing upon any of the world's great cities with an explosive force five times that of the bomb that destroyed Hiroshima.

The date was Aug. 10, 1972.

• • •

Spaceguard had been one of the last projects of the legendary NASA, at the close of the 20th century. Its initial objective had been modest enough: to make as complete a survey as possible of the asteroids and comets that crossed the orbit of Earth – and to determine if any were a potential threat.

With a total budget seldom exceeding $10 million a year, a world-wide network of telescopes, most of them operated by skilled amateurs, had been established by the year 2000. Sixty-one years later, the spectacular return of Halley's Comet* encouraged more funding, and the great 2079 fireball, luckily impacting in mid-Atlantic, gave Spaceguard additional prestige. By the end of the century, it had located more than one million asteroids, and the survey was believed to be 90% complete. However, it would have to be continued indefinitely: there was always a chance that some intruder might come rushing in from the uncharted outer reaches of the solar system.

As had Kali, which had been detected in late 2212 as it fell sunward past the orbit of Jupiter. Fortunately humankind had not been wholly unprepared, thanks to the fact that Senator George Ledstone (Independent, West America) had chaired an influential finance committee almost a generation earlier.

The Senator had one public eccentricity and, he cheerfully admitted, one secret vice. He always wore massive horn-rimmed eyeglasses (nonfunctional, of course) because they had an intimidating effect on uncooperative witnesses, few of whom had ever encountered such a novelty. His 'secret vice', perfectly well known to everyone, was rifle shooting on a standard Olympic range, set up in the tunnels of a long-abandoned missile silo near Mount Cheyenne. Ever since the demilitarization of Planet Earth (much accelerated by the famous slogan 'Guns Are the Crutches of the Impotent'), such activities had been frowned upon, though not actively discouraged.

There was no doubt that Senator Ledstone was an original; it seemed to run in the family. His grandmother had been a colonel in the dreaded Beverly Hills Militia, whose skirmishes with the L.A. Irregulars had spawned endless psychodramas in every medium, from old-fashioned ballet to direct brain stimulation. And his grandfather had been one of the most notorious bootleggers of the 21st century. Before he was killed in a shoot-out with the Canadian Medicops during an ingenious attempt to smuggle a kiloton of tobacco up Niagara Falls, it was estimated that 'Smokey' had been responsible for at least 20 million deaths.

Ledstone was quite unrepentant about his grandfather, whose sensational demise had triggered the repeal of the late U.S.'s third, and most disastrous, attempt at Prohibition. He argued that responsible adults should be allowed to commit suicide in any way they pleased – by alcohol, cocaine or even tobacco – as long as they did not kill innocent bystanders during the process.

When the proposed budget for Spaceguard Phase 2 was first presented to him, Senator Ledstone had been outraged by the idea of throwing billions of dollars into space. It was true that the global economy was in good shape; since the almost simultaneous collapse of communism and capitalism, the skillful application of chaos theory* by World Bank mathematicians had broken the old cycle of booms and busts and averted (so far) the Final Depression predicted by many pessimists. Nonetheless, the Senator argued that the money could be much better spent on Earth – especially on his favorite project, reconstructing what was left of California after the Superquake.

When Ledstone had twice vetoed Spaceguard Phase 2, everyone agreed that no one on Earth would make him change his mind. They had reckoned without someone from Mars.

The Red Planet was no longer quite so red, though the process of greening it had barely begun. Concentrating on the problems of survival, the colonists (they hated the word and were already saying proudly 'we Martians') had little energy left over for art or science. But the lightning flash of genius strikes where it will, and the greatest theoretical physicist of the century was born under the bubble domes of Port Lowell.

Like Einstein*, to whom he was often compared, Carlos Mendoza was an excellent musician; he owned the only saxophone on Mars and was a skilled performer on that antique instrument. He could have received his Nobel Prize* on Mars, as everyone expected, but he loved surprises and practical jokes. Thus he appeared in Stockholm looking like a knight in high-tech armor, wearing one of the powered exoskeletons developed for paraplegics. With this mechanical assistance, he could function almost unhandicapped in an environment that would otherwise have quickly killed him.

Needless to say, when the ceremony was over, Carlos was bombarded with invitations to scientific and social functions. Among the few he was able to accept was an appearance before the World Budget Committee, where Senator Ledstone closely questioned him about his opinion of Project Spaceguard.

'I live on a world which still bears the scars of a thousand meteor impacts, some of them *hundreds* of kilometers across,' said Professor Mendoza. 'Once they were equally common on Earth, but wind and rain – something we don't have yet on Mars, though we're working on it! – have worn them away.'

Senator Ledstone: 'The Spaceguarders are always pointing to signs of asteroid impacts on Earth. How seriously should we take their warnings?'

Professor Mendoza: 'Very seriously, Mr Chairman. Sooner or later, there's bound to be another major impact.'

Senator Ledstone was impressed, and indeed charmed, by the young scientist, but not yet convinced. What changed his mind was not a matter of logic but of emotion. On his way to London, Carlos Mendoza was killed in a bizarre accident when the control system of his exoskeleton malfunctioned. Deeply moved, Ledstone immediately dropped his opposition to Spaceguard, approving construction of two powerful orbiting tugs, *Goliath* and *Titan*, to be kept permanently patrolling on opposite sides of the sun. And when he was a very old man, he said to one of his aides, 'They tell me we'll soon be able to take Mendoza's brain out of that tank of liquid nitrogen, and talk to it through a computer interface. I wonder what he's been thinking about, all these years . . .'

• • •

Assembled on Phobos, the inner satellite of Mars, ATLAS was little more than a set of rocket engines attached to propellant tanks holding 100,000 tons of hydrogen. Though its fusion drive could generate far less thrust than the primitive missile that had carried Yuri Gagarin* into space, it could run continuously not merely for minutes but for weeks. Even so, the effect on the asteroid would be trivial, a velocity change of a few centimeters per second. Yet that might be sufficient to deflect Kali from its fatal orbit during the months while it was still falling earthward.

• • •

Now that ATLAS's propellant tanks, control systems and thrusters had been securely mounted on Kali, it looked as if some lunatic had built an oil refinery on an asteroid. Captain Singh was exhausted, as were all the crew members, after days of assembly and checking. Yet he felt a warm glow of achievement: they had done everything that was expected of them, the countdown was going smoothly, and the rest was up to ATLAS.

He would have been far less relaxed had he known of the ABSOLUTE PRIORITY message racing toward him by tight infrared beam from ASTROPOL headquarters in Geneva. It would not reach *Goliath* for another 30 minutes. And by then it would be much too late.

• • •

At about T minus 30 minutes*, *Goliath* had drawn away from Kali to stand well clear of the jet with which ATLAS would try to nudge it from its present course. 'Like a mouse pushing an elephant,' one media person had described the operation. But in the frictionless vacuum of space, where momentum could never be lost, even one mousepower would be enough if applied early and over a sufficient length of time.

The group of officers waiting quietly on the bridge did not expect to see anything spectacular: the plasma jet of the ATLAS drive would be far too hot to produce much visible radiation. Only the telemetry would confirm that ignition had started and that Kali was no longer an implacable juggernaut, wholly beyond the control of humanity.

There was a brief round of cheering and a gentle patter of applause as the string of zeros on the accelerometer display began to change. The feeling on the bridge was one of relief rather than exultation. Though Kali was stirring, it would be days and weeks before victory was assured.

And then, unbelievably, the numbers dropped back to zero. Seconds later, three simultaneous audio alarms sounded. All eyes were suddenly fixed on Kali and the ATLAS booster which should be nudging it from its present course. The sight was heartbreaking: the great propellant tanks were opening up like flowers in a time-lapse movie, spilling out the thousands of tons of reaction mass that might have saved the Earth. Wisps of vapor drifted across the face of the asteroid, veiling its cratered surface with an evanescent atmosphere.

Then Kali continued along its path, heading inexorably toward a fiery collision with the Earth.

• • •

Captain Singh was alone in the large, well-appointed cabin that had been his home for longer than any other place in the solar system. He was still dazed but was trying to make his peace with the universe.

He had lost, finally and forever, all that he loved on Earth. With the decline of the nuclear family, he had known many deep attachments, and it had been hard to decide who should be the mothers of the two children he was permitted. A phrase from an old American novel (he had forgotten the author) kept coming into his mind: 'Remember them as they were – and write them off.' The fact that he himself was perfectly safe somehow made him feel worse; *Goliath* was in no danger whatsoever, and still had all the propellant it needed to rejoin the shaken survivors of humanity on the Moon or Mars.

Well, he had many friendships – and one that was much more than that – on Mars; this was where his future must lie. He was only 102, with decades of active life ahead of him. But some of the crew had loved ones on the Moon; he would have to put *Goliath*'s destination to the vote.

Ship's Orders had never covered a situation like this.

• • •

'I still don't understand,' said the chief engineer, 'why that explosive cord wasn't detected on the preflight check-out.'

'Because that Reborn fanatic could have hidden it easily – and no one would have dreamed of looking for such a thing. Pity ASTROPOL didn't catch him while he was still on Phobos.'

'But *why* did they do it? I can't believe that even Chrislamic crazies would want to destroy the Earth.'

'You can't argue with their logic – if you accept their premises. God, Allah, is testing us, and we mustn't interfere. If Kali misses, fine. If it doesn't, well, that's part of Her bigger plan. Maybe we've messed up Earth so badly that it's time to start over. Remember that old saying of Tsiolkovski's: "Earth is the cradle of humankind, but you cannot live in the cradle forever." Kali could be a sign that it's time to leave.'

The captain held up his hand for silence.

'The only important question now is, Moon or Mars? They'll

both need us. I don't want to influence you' (that was hardly true; everyone knew where he wanted to go), 'so I'd like your views first.'

The first ballot was Mars – six, Moon – six, Don't know – one, captain abstaining.

Each side was trying to convert the single 'Don't know' when David spoke.

'There is an alternative.'

'What do you mean?' Captain Singh demanded, rather brusquely.

'It seems obvious. Even though ATLAS is destroyed, we still have a chance of saving the Earth. According to my calculations, *Goliath* has just enough propellant to deflect Kali – if we start thrusting against it immediately. But the longer we wait, the less the probability of success.'

There was a moment of stunned silence on the bridge as everyone asked the question, 'Why didn't I think of that?' and quickly arrived at the answer.

David had kept his head, if one could use so inappropriate a phrase, while all the humans around him were in a state of shock. There were some compensations in being a Legal Person (Nonhuman). Though David could not know love, neither could he know fear. He would continue to think logically, even to the edge of doom.

• • •

With any luck, thought Captain Singh, this is my last broadcast to Earth. I'm tired of being a hero, and a slightly premature one at that. Many things could still go wrong, as indeed they already have . . .

'This is Captain Singh, space tug *Goliath*. First of all, let me say how glad we are that the Elders of Chrislam have identified the saboteurs and handed them over to ASTROPOL.

'We are now fifty days from Earth, and we have a slight problem. This one, I hasten to add, will not affect our new attempt to deflect Kali into a safe orbit. I note that the news media are calling this

deflection Operation Deliverance. We like the name, and hope to
live up to it, but we still cannot be absolutely certain of success. David,
who appreciates all the goodwill messages he has received, estimates
that the probability of Kali impacting Earth is still 10% . . .

'We had intended to keep just enough propellant reserve to leave
Kali shortly before encounter and go into a safer orbit, where our
sister ship *Titan* could rendezvous with us. But that option is now
closed. While *Goliath* was pushing against Kali at maximum drive,
we broke through a weak point in the crust. The ship wasn't
damaged, but we're stuck! All attempts to break away have failed.

'We're not worried, and it may even be a blessing in disguise.
Now we'll use the *whole* of our remaining propellant to give one
final nudge. Perhaps that will be the last drop that's needed to do
the job. So we'll ride Kali past Earth, and wave to you from a
comfortable distance, in just fifty days.'

It would be the longest fifty days in the history of the world.

• • •

Now the huge crescent of the Moon spanned the sky, the jagged
mountain peaks along the terminator burning with the fierce light
of the lunar dawn. But the dusty plains still untouched by the sun
were not completely dark; they were glowing faintly in the light
reflected from Earth's clouds and continents. And scattered here
and there across that once dead landscape were the glowing fireflies
that marked the first permanent settlements humankind had built
beyond the home planet. Captain Singh could easily locate Clavius
Base, Port Armstrong, Plato City. He could even see the necklace of
faint lights along the Translunar Railroad, bringing its precious cargo
of water from the ice mines at the South Pole.

Earth was now only five hours away.

• • •

Kali entered Earth's atmosphere soon after local midnight, 200km
above Hawaii. Instantly, the gigantic fireball brought a false dawn

to the Pacific, awakening the wildlife on its myriad islands. But few humans had been asleep this night of nights, except those who had sought the oblivion of drugs.

Over New Zealand, the heat of the orbiting furnace ignited forests and melted the snow on mountaintops, triggering avalanches into the valleys beneath. But the human race had been very, very lucky: the main thermal impact as Kali passed the Earth was on the Antarctic, the continent that could best absorb it. Even Kali could not strip away all the kilometers of polar ice, but it set in motion the Great Thaw that would change coastlines all around the world.

No one who survived hearing it could ever describe the sound of Kali's passage; none of the recordings were more than feeble echoes. The video coverage, of course, was superb, and would be watched in awe for generations to come. But nothing could ever compare with the fearsome reality.

Two minutes after it had sliced into the atmosphere, Kali re-entered space. Its closest approach to Earth had been 60km. In that two minutes, it took 100,000 lives and did $1 trillion worth of damage.

• • •

Goliath had been protected from the fireball by the massive shield of Kali itself; the sheets of incandescent plasma streamed harmlessly overhead. But when the asteroid smashed into Earth's blanket of air at more than 100 times the speed of sound, the colossal drag forces mounted swiftly to five, ten, twenty gravities – and peaked at a level far beyond anything that machines or flesh could withstand.

Now indeed Kali's orbit had been drastically changed; never again would it come near Earth. On its next return to the inner solar system, the swifter spacecraft of a later age would visit the crumpled wreckage of *Goliath* and bear reverently homeward the bodies of those who had saved the world.

Until the next encounter.

NOTES

zero-G (p143)

zero gravity

David and Goliath (p143)

Goliath was a Philistine giant, according to legend killed by the boy David (later King of Israel in the 10th century BC)

Kali (p144)

the name of the Hindu goddess of destruction and death

Chrislam (p145)

the author's invented compound word for a new religion

New Dead Sea Scrolls (p145)

the original scrolls were ancient manuscripts, containing texts of the Bible's Old Testament, discovered in caves near the Dead Sea

Cold Fusion (p145)

the union at room temperatures (instead of very high ones) of atomic nuclei to form a heavier nucleus, causing the release of energy; the validity of this process is still in doubt at present

'One small step for a man . . . (p145)

. . . one giant leap for mankind'; words spoken by Neil Armstrong, the first man to set foot on the moon in 1969

Halley's Comet (p147)

a bright comet, first recorded in 240 BC, that returns to the inner solar system about every 76 years; it was last seen in 1986

chaos theory (p148)

a modern scientific theory that says small random events can have disproportionately far-reaching effects; e.g. a butterfly flaps its wings in the Amazon rain forest, causing a hurricane in India

Einstein (p149)

Albert Einstein (1879–1955), German-born US theoretical physicist, founder of the theory of relativity and one of the greatest scientists of the 20th century

Nobel Prize (p149)

prizes, endowed by the Swedish chemist Alfred Nobel, awarded annually for outstanding achievement in chemistry, physics, medicine, literature, and the promotion of peace

Yuri Gagarin (p150)

Russian cosmonaut, the first man in space in 1961

T minus 30 minutes (p150)

30 minutes before time on target

DISCUSSION

1   Do you think *The Hammer of God* is an appropriate title for this story? Why, or why not? What other titles can you think of that would be suitable?

2   In an interview in 1993, Arthur C. Clarke said he firmly believed that two of the technologies in this story, virtual reality and cold fusion, would exist in the future. Virtual reality, already available in a primitive form, would allow people to experience, through equipment fitted on the head, very realistic images and sounds created by computer. Cold fusion, if it works, could remove the need to burn coal, oil, gas or use nuclear fission to produce power. Do you think these two technologies would benefit humankind? Why, or why not?

3   Some scientists regard the threat of an impact by a comet or asteroid as a very real one. A recent report, titled Spaceguard, to the United States Congress, proposed that a survey be done to find out whether any large comets are in orbits likely to cross Earth's. The estimated cost would be 300 million dollars. Do you think that would be money well spent, or would it be better spent on protection from floods, earthquakes, hurricanes, and other natural disasters?

LANGUAGE FOCUS

1   Look at the following words from the text. As with some of the other stories, these words are based on existing words but are used to suggest things or people or inventions that don't (yet) exist. Use your imagination, and clues from the story, to write descriptions of them.

> *Skylift Service* (p142)
> *robotoys* (p143)
> *spacer* (p144)
> *the portable 'Brainman'* (p144)
> *neural programming* (p145)
> *psychodramas* (p148)
> *Medicops* (p148)
> *Superquake* (p148)
> *exoskeleton* (p149)

2   'Guns are the crutches of the impotent.' How would you express this idea in your own words? Do you think it is an effective slogan? Think

of some things that you approve or disapprove of, and try to invent similar slogans, using metaphors like 'crutches' in the same way. For example:

Books are the nourishment for the mind.
Money is the root of all evil.
Education is the path to power.

3   The last part of Captain Singh's final broadcast to Earth is expressed in a very casual and understated way, reassuring to his audience; he talks of being 'not worried' and 'waving from a comfortable distance'. But the position of the crew of the *Goliath* is actually one of heroic self-sacrifice. Rewrite the last part of the speech from 'We're not worried...' in a way that expresses directly the gravity of the situation and the emotions that the Captain and his crew must be feeling.

ACTIVITIES

1   Imagine that you were there, and survived, the impact of Kali on the Earth's atmosphere. How did you spend what might have been your last few hours alive? What did you do after Kali had passed? Write your diary for the twelve hours before and after the event.

2   The story contains an enormous number of ideas, often mentioned in passing, about how the world and human society might be in the future. The ideas cover politics, religion, the family, style and fashion, recreation and entertainment, government, militarization... Do you think all the ideas are positive ones? Make a list of as many as you can find, and use your notes to write a short description of society in the 23rd century. Would you like to live in such a world?

3   Did you like this story? Why, or why not? Write a review of it for a newspaper or a magazine.

QUESTIONS FOR DISCUSSION OR WRITING

1   Several of these stories contain aliens of one kind or another. Which did you find most interesting, and why? Do you think the authors have portrayed them as physically different, but with mostly human characteristics? Imagine that you are an alien from one of these stories, and write a letter to your home planet, describing human beings from your point of view.

2   Most of the human characters in these stories are faced with dangers or predicaments outside our current experience. What typical human characteristics did they show in reacting to their circumstances? Write brief character sketches of some of them, summarizing what you think are their good or bad points. Which of them did you feel most sympathy for? Why?

3   Look at the two stories about machines and the human race's relationship with them. Are the machines shown as dominant, or human beings? Do you think it is ever likely that we will be 'enslaved' by machines, or unable to survive without them? The pace of technological change has been very fast in this century, and is likely to continue in the future. Do you think all technological progress is good? Make a list of the dangers and benefits as you see them, in relation to the circumstances of your own country.

4   What kinds of future society are portrayed in the stories *Zero Hour, Human Is, Who Can Replace a Man?* and *The Hammer of God*? Are they optimistic or pessimistic pictures? Write a short review, comparing the four stories, and saying which social changes seem to you to be the most likely or desirable.

5   Some might say that science fiction is only a kind of modern fairy-tale, providing escapist fantasies, a long way from reality. Others say that science fiction is a tremendous vehicle for ideas – social, political, religious, philosophical, psychological, and so on – all of which relate to the human condition. Brian Aldiss, in his history of science fiction, argued that 'science fiction is the search for a definition of humanity and its status in the universe which will stand in our advanced but confused state of knowledge'.

   Which opinion do you agree with? How do the stories in this volume, or any other science fiction stories you have read, support your view?

6   Have you seen any science-fiction films or television series, made in your
    own country, or elsewhere? For example:

    2001: A Space Odyssey
    Blade Runner
    E.T.: The Extraterrestial
    Star Trek
    Dr Who
    Jurassic Park

    Did you find them entertaining, frightening, interesting, silly? Do you
    think science fiction works best in films or in books? Why?
        Would any of the stories in this volume make a good film? Choose
    one, and write a short description of the kind of film you would make
    (humorous, frightening, etc.), and what production difficulties there
    would be.